HOW TO USE THIS BOOK

Your Collins Traveller Guide will help you find your way around your holiday destination quickly and easily. It is split into two sections which are colour-coded:

The blue section provides you with an alphabetical sequence of headings, from **ART GALLERIES** to **WALKS** via **EXCURSIONS**, **RESTAURANTS**, **SHOPPING**, etc. Each entry within a topic includes information on how to get there, how much it will cost you, when it will be open and what to expect. Furthermore, every page has its own map showing the position of each item and the nearest landmark. This allows you to orientate yourself quickly and easily in your new surroundings.

To find what you want to do – having dinner, visiting a museum, going for a walk or shopping for gifts – simply flick through the blue headings and take your pick!

The red section is an alphabetical list of information. It provides essential facts about places and cultural items – 'What are *bastide* towns?', 'When is the Sigoulès wine fair?', 'Where is Nontron?' – and expands on subjects touched on in the first half of the book. This section also contains practical travel information. It ranges through how to find accommodation, where to hire a car, the variety of eating places and food available, tips on health, information on money, which newspapers are available, how to find a taxi and where the Youth Hostels are. It is lively and informative and easy to use. Each band shows the first three letters of the first entry on the page. Simply flick through the bands till you find the entry you need!

All the main entries are also cross-referenced to help you find them. Names in small capitals – **CHILDREN** – tell you that there is more information about the item you are looking for under the topic on children in the first part of the book. So when you read 'see **CHILDREN**' you turn to the blue heading for **CHILDREN**. The instruction 'see **A-Z**', after a word, lets you know that the word has its own entry in the second part of the book. Similarly words in bold type – **Lascaux** – also let you know that there is an entry in the gazetteer for the indicated name. In both cases you just look under the appropriate heading in the red section. Packed full of information and easy to use – you'll always know where you are with your Collins Traveller Guide!

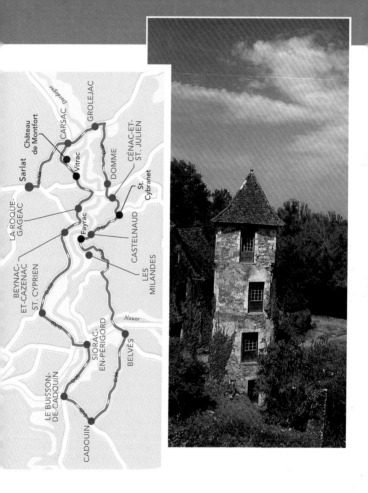

Sarlat
Château
de Montfort
CARSAC
CÉNAC-ET-
ST. JULIEN
Vitrac
DOMME
GROLEJAC
CÉNAC-ET-
ST. JULIEN
St.
Cybranet
Fayrac
CASTELNAUD
LA ROQUE-
GAGEAC
LES
MILANDES
BEYNAC-
ET-CAZENAC
ST. CYPRIEN
SIORAC-
EN-PÉRIGORD
BELVÈS
LE BUISSON-
DE-CADOUIN
CADOUIN
Nauze
Dordogne

INTRODUCTION

France may one day exist no more, but the Dordogne will live on just as dreams live on and nourish the souls of men,' wrote Henry Miller in the dark days of World War II.

The two neighbouring departments of the Dordogne and the Lot are possibly the most beautiful in France, and, once visited, will never be forgotten. The region, which is steeped in prehistory – man was very active here 40,000 years ago – covers an area roughly rectangular of about 120 km northwest-southeast and 80 km northeast-southwest. There are few towns of significance: Périgueux, Bergerac and Sarlat in the Dordogne, and Cahors, Figeac and Gourdon in the Lot, but part of the area's great charm lies in the hundreds of little villages and hamlets nestling in the river valleys. Round each corner – and all the roads are superbly maintained – lies a surprise: a 12thC Romanesque church or a mildly battered chateau hold court; half-timbered medieval houses fringe the central *place* where, under the plane or chestnut trees, an amiable game of *boules* is being played. The morning open-air market is closing down as housewives contemplate last-minute purchases, and the *patron* of the local restaurant is pouring out a glass of Bergerac *rouge* while Madame is cutting the vegetables for her *crudités* – the first of four or five courses on the lunch menu.

The villages are the living heart of the region. Parts of Henry Miller's dreams must have been of the medieval hamlets of Carennac and Autoire, St. Jean-de-Côle and St. Léon-de-Vézère, and of course St. Cirq-Lapopie. Every visitor will find his or her favourite among the excursions in this book.

If the villages are the living heart then the rivers are the arteries. The great blue-green rivers of the Dordogne and the Lot bisect the region as they flow majestically from the east towards Bordeaux and the Atlantic. Yet, in some ways the score of smaller rivers – the Bave and Céré, the L'Isle and the Vézère – have even more charm. It is the rivers and thousands of acres of woodland that give the region a marvellous, equable climate that attracts many thousands of visitors to spend their summer holidays here or to purchase retirement homes. The air is astonishingly pure, there is little pollution and visitors will notice road signs urging everyone to keep the place *propre*, i.e. clean and tidy.

The historic links between Britain and the regions known for nearly

2000 years as Périgord and Quercy extend back for centuries. It wasn't until 1790 that the parliamentary bureaucrats decided that historical and sentimental names were out and pragmatic river-named departments were in, so La Dordogne and Le Lot were created – not that the locals take much heed!

When Eleanor of Aquitaine married Henry Plantagenet in 1152 her dowry included Périgord, the region round Périgueux. In 1190 Richard Coeur de Lion, her swashbuckling son, signed an agreement with the French King Philippe Auguste whereby neighbouring Quercy, with its capital town of Cahors, was ceded to the English throne. Nearly 70 years later, at the Treaty of Paris in 1259, King St. Louis of France conceded ownership of Périgord and Quercy to King Edward I. At the same time the two kings built or strengthened the defences of the frontier castles, such as Beynac and Castelnaud, which glared at each other across the River Dordogne. For commercial, social and political reasons they also built over a hundred *bastide* towns near rivers, enabling *gabares* (flat-bottomed boats with sails) to trade in wine and produce, or on main roads (perhaps on the many pilgrim routes to Santiago de Compostela in Spain which traverse the region) to attract commerce. A dozen of these *bastide* towns still exist – they are very interesting archi-

tecturally – at, for instance, Monpazier, Domme and Beaumont.
The three centuries of English rule brought alternate periods of prosperity and ruin to the region. The three most dramatic historical personages were also perhaps the most harmful: Richard Coeur de Lion who, apart from hunting in the forests or carousing with his troubadour friends in the feudal 'courts of love', preferred above all to destroy castles, which he did once too often, perishing at Chalus in 1191; Simon de Montfort, who invaded Périgord and Quercy with just one purpose – to put to death the Albigensian 'heretics'; and Edward the Black Prince who, with his military *chevauchées* of 1355, totally destroyed the wretched peasantry and their villages.

When Edward III proclaimed himself so arrogantly King of France, it was not surprising that the French King Jean II declared war in Aquitaine with the taking of Domme in 1347. A century later Sir John Talbot and his English army were defeated at Castillon-la-Bataille (west of Bergerac), ending the famous Hundred Years' War.

The next century was peaceful until the Reformation of the Church spread to Aquitaine. Jean Chauvin (1509-64) brought Calvinism and the Huguenot faith to the region. By 1540 Bergerac, La Force and Ste-Foy-La-Grande were bastions of the beliefs originated by Martin Luther.

Soon the Catholic Church retaliated, and in 1562 Protestants were slaughtered in Cahors. At the Massacre of St. Bartholomew ten years later, thousands of Huguenots were killed and the great exodus began that was to continue until after the revocation of the Edict of Nantes in 1685. About 10,000 families emigrated to England and the Netherlands *pour cause de religion*, and Aquitaine, like the rest of France, lost many of its ablest citizens, not only silk-weavers, gold and silversmiths and skilled artisans, but also bankers, lawyers and the military. It is indicative of the local character to remember that *les Croquants*, the peasants involved in the rebellions against the oppressive landlords of the late 16thC, were succeeded in the mid-20thC by the Resistance groups of Périgord and Quercy who fought so bravely against their Teuton 'landlords'. Scores of the modern martyrs are remembered on plaques in village squares and on the memorial to the Resistance on the N 20 north of Cahors.

The region offers superlative outdoor holidays for the family, especially children. The rivers and their environs provide camp sites, canoes for rental, safe swimming (also in lakes, *piscines* and man-made *plans d'eau*), fishing, horse riding, splendid walks along the Grandes Randonnées and, above all, tennis and cycling.

There are scores of camp sites and dozens of modest hotels in both departments, where a room for two costs as little as 100F, but pre-booking for the summer season is advisable.

Cultural opportunities abound. There are music festivals – classical,

jazz and blues – at Bergerac, Cahors, Bonaguil, Souillac, St. Céré and Brantôme. There is a pantomime festival at Périgueux, a theatre festival at Sarlat, distinguished abbeys and churches to visit at Cadouin, Brantôme, Périgueux and Cahors – even a pilgrimage to Rocamadour. A wide range of museums caters for a variety of tastes, from bees, truffles, butterflies and monkeys to tapestries, sacred art, folklore and wine. Among the attractions children will enjoy are the Gramat Safari Park, the toy museum at Nontron, vintage cars at St. Céré and mechanical toys at Souillac. Children of all ages will want to visit some of the prehistoric grottoes around Les Eyzies-de-Tayac and Montignac, and the caves or chasms of Padirac and Lacave – among many others mentioned in several excursions.

Wine lovers especially will be interested in the five AOC (Appellation d'Origine Contrôllée) areas round Bergerac as well as a visit to the Château de Monbazillac, and a trip further south to taste the 'black wines' of Cahors at Parnac.

The first thing to do on a holiday in the Dordogne and the Lot is to contact the efficient and helpful Tourist Offices and obtain the list of local fetes, *foires*, *expositions* or *manifestations*, and the second is to visit an open market to see the gamut of edibles – foie gras, herbs and cheeses, freshwater fish, walnut oil, *cèpes* (mushrooms), chestnuts, truffles and colourful fruit and vegetables – that will appear on local menus.

At the end of your holiday you could put Henry Miller's dreams to the test and consult the A-Z under the heading 'House Purchase'. Bon voyage.

Pont Valentré

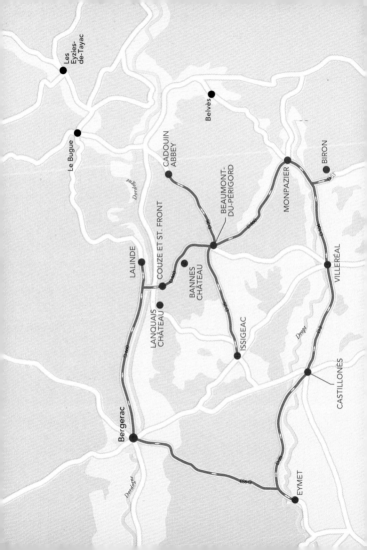

Les Eyzies-de-Tayac

Belvès

Le Bugue

CADOUIN ABBEY

BEAUMONT-DU-PÉRIGORD

MONPAZIER

BIRON

Dordogne

COUZE ET ST. FRONT

LALINDE

VILLERÉAL

BANNES CHÂTEAU

LANQUAIS CHÂTEAU

ISSIGEAC

Dropt

CASTILLONÈS

Bergerac

Dordogne

EYMET

A one-day excursion to the bastide *towns to the southeast. Although there are 18* bastide *towns (see* **A-Z***) within 40 km of Bergerac, many of them are not worth visiting, as 'modernization' has destroyed much of the original unique gridiron defensive townships. Vergt, Villefranche-de-Lonchat, Fonroque, Roquepine and Puyguilhem come into this category.*

From Bergerac cross the river and head south on the D 933.

25 km – Eymet (pop: 3000) is becoming popular with British property buyers. If you are not interested in wines, you could look at two fine chateaux en route: the 16thC Monbazillac chateau which houses a Protestant History museum (see **CHATEAUX-BERGERAC**), and 15thC Bridoire, which is unfortunately not open to the public. Unusually for a *bastide* town founded in 1271, Eymet has the remains of a small 14thC chateau, which houses a folklore and prehistory museum (1000-1200, 1500-1900 exc. Sun. am, mid June-mid Sep., rest of year pm only: 10F). The restaurants Beauséjour and Du Château serve locally pro-duced rich goose and duck liver. Drive 18 km to the east by cross-country minor roads.

43 km – Castillonès is another small *bastide* town, bisected by the N 21. Villeréal is also a small *bastide* town with the River Dropt mean-dering parallel to the D 2, 13 km from Castillonès. Drive 16 km east via the D 104.

72 km – Biron is one of the most interesting chateaux in the Aquitaine region, and is definitely worth a 1-hr guided tour to see the well-restored fortress and Renaissance chateau. Each generation added a dif-ferent architectural style, but the whole is magnificent (see **CHATEAUX-BERGERAC**). Drive 8 km north via the D 53 and D 104.

80 km – Monpazier is the best-preserved example of a *bastide* town in the region. King Edward I founded it in 1284 and it is still much as it was then – gridiron streets, gates, towers, covered arcades and the forti-fied church of St. Dominique. The 13thC chapterhouse is near the church. Ancient weight and grain measures can be seen in the market-place. Monpazier has several good restaurants including De France and La Bastide. Drive 16 km northwest on the D 660.

96 km – Beaumont-du-Périgord is another 'English' *bastide*, built in 1272. The 13thC fortified church of St. Front, market square and hall,

and strong Luzier gateway still remain intact, and the streets are straight and wide.

There are various alternatives now: a visit northeast to Cadouin abbey (see **SARLAT-EXCURSION 2**); a trip west to Issigeac, a pretty village with a 17thC bishop's castle (now the Hôtel de Ville), a Gothic 16thC church and several medieval timber-framed houses amid narrow, twisting streets; or north via the D 660 past 15thC Bannes Château with its machicolated towers (closed to the public) and the village of Couze et St. Front. 2 km west on the D 37 is Lanquais Château, built in the 15thC and well worth a visit (see **CHATEAUX-BERGERAC**). Finally there is Lalinde, an English *bastide* town founded in 1270, with a rectangular pattern of streets, some ramparts and a western gate. From the public gardens there are delightful views of the River Dordogne.

It is 29 km west on the D 660 from Beaumont-du-Périgord to Bergerac.

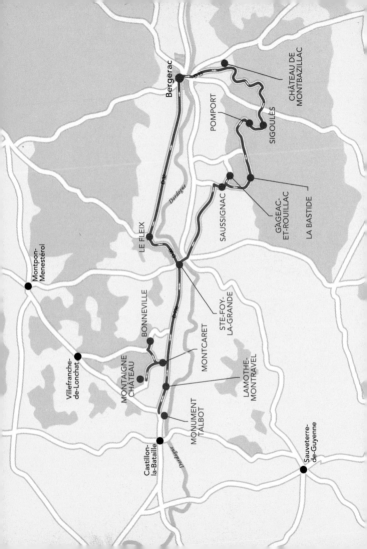

Excursion 2

A one-day wine tour.

Cross the river bridge and drive south on the D 13.

7 km – Château Monbazillac (see **CHATEAUX-BERGERAC**). Built in 1550, the wine co-operative which owns the chateau has restored it with great care. Across the courtyard is a good restaurant and separate wine-tasting and buying salon. As well as the remarkable, very sweet, golden-yellow wine with a superb aroma (look for Château Monbazillac, Grande Réserve or Château Septy), you will find that the co-op produces all the Bergerac range of wines. Next go south and west cross-country past Bridoire castle, across the D 933 to Pomport and Sigoulès (which has three excellent restaurants). Both villages also have wine co-ops. Drive a short distance to the north.

25 km – La Bastide has the remains of an English-built *bastide* (see **A-Z**). Carry on to the little village of Saussignac. The large 16thC chateau is privately owned. There are several wine growers here who produce the unusual white Côtes de Saussignac wines. 2 km to the east is the village of Gageac-et-Rouillac with its 14thC chateau, which is privately owned, and medieval houses. Now drive by minor roads 7 km northwest.

34 km – Ste-Foy-La-Grande (pop: 3400), a ramparted small town which was built as a French *bastide* in 1255. The rectangular grid of streets is on the south side of the River Dordogne. It is a centre for the AOC Montravel and Côtes de Montravel wine growers, although the villages to visit lie just to the west, in a rectangle 20 km by 10 km. There are wine co-ops in Montcaret, Bonneville and Lamothe-Montravel just north of the D 936. The famous St. Emilion wine area is 18 km to the west and Montaigne's chateau is close to the wine villages (see **CHATEAUX-BERGERAC**). The monument to General Talbot, who commanded the British army which was defeated in 1453, thereby ending the Hundred Years' War, lies between Lamothe-Montravel and Castillon-la-Bataille (where the battle was fought). Return east to Bergerac by the quieter country roads following the northern bank of the River Dordogne, the D 20 and D 32, some 25 km from Ste-Foy-La-Grande. On the way look at the pretty village of Le Fleix with its medieval houses and modern artisans.

Pl. Gambetta

LE CYRANO

Pl. J. Ferry

rue Sainte Catherine

Pl. de la République

rue du Dr Breton

rue des Carmes

LE TERROIR

Pl. de Lattre de Tassigny

rue Mounet Sully

rue de la Résistance

ROYAL-PÉRIGORD

rue Bourbarraud

LE ST. JAMES

rue du Mourrier

Grande Rue

rue du Colonel de Chabois

LE PARISIEN

Pl. du Marché Couvert

Pl. des Petites Boucheries

rue P. Bert

rue Neuve d'Argenson

Pl. Malbec

rue du Prof. Pozzi

rue Saint James

rue des Fontaines

L'ENFANCE DE LARD

Pl. Pélissière

LE MENU PLAISIR

rue des Conférences

Pl. Doublet

rue Junien Rabier

Pl. de la Myrpe

Pl. du Docteur Cayla

rue Neuve d'Argenson

rue Candillac

rue du Port

rue de l'Ancien Pont

St. Clair

LE NAUTIC

LE ST. CLAR

rue du Château

Dordogne

Restaurants

LE CYRANO 2 Bd Montaigne, in hotel of same name.
❏ 1200-1400, 1930-2100 Tue.-Sat., 1200-1400 Sun. ❏ Expensive.
Hotel in park, with classic French cuisine and Pécharmont red wines.

LE TERROIR (Hotel de Bordeaux), 38 Pl. Gambetta.
❏ 1200-1400, 1900-2100. Closed mid Dec.-late Jan. ❏ Expensive.
Good Périgourdin cuisine. Try the confits and foie gras.

L'ENFANCE DE LARD Pl. Pélissière.
❏ 1200-1400, 2000-2130 Mon.-Sat. ❏ Expensive.
Rich Périgourdin cuisine and grills, confits, foie gras and local wines.

LE PARISIEN rue de la Fonbalquine, near the covered market.
❏ 1200-1400, 1900-2100 Tue.-Sat., 1200-1400 Sun. Closed mid Oct.-
mid Nov. ❏ Moderate.
Typical rich cuisine du Périgord served on a shady terrace.

LE NAUTIC 12-14 Promenade Pierre Loti.
❏ 1200-1400, 1900-2100 Tue.-Sun. Closed Nov. ❏ Moderate.
Good river trout and écrevisses served with white Monbazillac wine.

LE ST. CLAR 4 rue Neuve d'Argenson.
❏ 1200-1400, 1900-2100. ❏ Moderate.
Good-value prix fixe menus and local wines.

ROYAL-PÉRIGORD 19-21 rue de la Résistance, north of old town.
❏ 1200-1400, 1500-2100. Closed Sun. out of season. ❏ Inexpensive.
Restaurant, brasserie, bar, salon de thé and good pâtisserie.

LE MENU PLAISIR 39 rue Neuve d'Argenson.
❏ 1200-1400, 1900-2100 Tue.-Sat., 1200-1400 Sun. ❏ Inexpensive.
The specialities here are the river fish dishes.

LE ST. JAMES 81 rue Neuve d'Argenson.
❏ 1200-1400, 1500-2045 Tue.-Sun. ❏ Inexpensive.
A restaurant, pub and salon de thé all in one.

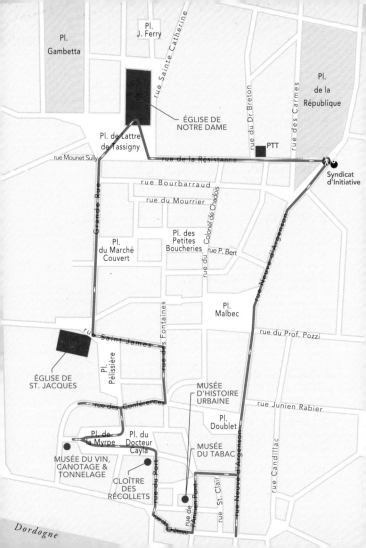

Pl. Gambetta

Pl. J. Ferry

rue Sainte Catherine

Pl. de la République

rue du Dr Breton

rue des Carmes

ÉGLISE DE NOTRE DAME

Pl. de Lattre de Tassigny

rue Mounet Sully

rue de la Résistance

PTT

Syndicat d'Initiative

rue Bourbarraud

rue du Mourrier

Grande Rue

rue du Colonel de Chadois

Pl. du Marché Couvert

Pl. des Petites Boucheries

rue P. Bert

Pl. Malbec

rue Neuve d'Argenson

rue du Prof. Pozzi

rue Saint James

rue des Fontaines

ÉGLISE DE ST. JACQUES

Pl. Pélissière

rue des Conférences

MUSÉE D'HISTOIRE URBAINE

rue Junien Rabier

Pl. Doublet

Pl. de la Myrpe

Pl. du Docteur Cayla

MUSÉE DU TABAC

MUSÉE DU VIN, CANOTAGE & TONNELAGE

CLOÎTRE DES RÉCOLLETS

rue du Port

rue de l'Ancien Pont

Vieux Château

rue St. Clair

rue Candillac

Dordogne

Walk

2 hr.

For three centuries, until 1450, this town was ruled from London. Your ancestors may have walked these streets. Start at the Tourist Office, at 97 rue Neuve d'Argenson in the triangular Pl. de la République at the north end of Bergerac. Walk west past the PTT (post office) in the rue de la Résistance for 350 m to the 19thC Église de Notre Dame (see **BERGERAC-WHAT TO SEE**). Two paintings by Italian artists and, in the West chapel, a large Aubusson tapestry, are worth a look. Head south towards the river down the Grande Rue to the Pl. du Marché Couvert. Beside the market hall (market days are Wed. and Sat. am) are a 16thC grocer's shop and remains of the town ramparts. Keep on along the Grande Rue to see the Église de St. Jacques (see **BERGERAC-WHAT TO SEE**) with an attractive window and arched belfry. The church was named after pilgrims on their way to St. Jacques of Compostela. The rue Saint-James at the north end of the square leads to the rue des Fontaines and rue Gaudra. In both streets there are 15th, 16th and 17thC town houses, the *vieille auberges*, and ornamental arcades and cornices from the 14thC. The rue des Conférences leads back to the Pl. Pélissière, so called because the peace treaty of Bergerac was signed here in 1577. Look at the old wattle and daub houses, the Duc d'Epernon's house and the Musée d'Art Sacré (see **BERGERAC-WHAT TO SEE**). One of Bergerac's citizens – the long-nosed, bibulous, romantic Cyrano de Bergerac – is on view in the middle of the Pl. de la Myrpe. The mythical hero of Edmond Rostand's play was the 17thC philosopher of the same name, who had nothing to do with Bergerac! At the west end of the Pl. de la Myrpe is the interesting Musée du Vin, Canotage & Tonnelage (see **BERGERAC-WHAT TO SEE**). For centuries wines from Bergerac were shipped to England, and from Monbazillac to Holland. The *gabares*, flat-bottomed boats with sails, carried them down-river to Bordeaux for transhipment overseas. Bergerac was indeed an inland commercial 'port' of substance.

Retrace your footsteps east through the Pl. du Docteur Cayla, down the rue du Port towards the Cloître des Récollets, the HQ of the Interprofessional Council for Bergerac Wines (see **BERGERAC-WHAT TO SEE**). Partly 16thC, partly 18thC, the cloisters housed the Protestant temple. Known as Huguenots (see **A-Z**), many thousands of Protestants left

Bergerac in the 16th and 17thC for England and Holland to seek religious sanctuary. There is a fine vaulted cellar, and stone staircases lead to council rooms with views over the river to the south, of the Bergerac and Monbazillac vineyards. The rue du Château and rue de l'Ancien-Port lead to the two museums in the interesting corner building, Maison Peyrarède. Even nonsmokers will find the unique tobacco museum fascinating, with its display of Indian peace pipes, snuffboxes, ancient cigarette holders, tobacco graters, porcelain jars, meerschaums and, on the second floor, a collection of paintings depicting smokers of yore (see **BERGERAC-WHAT TO SEE**). The next-door house, Musée d'Histoire Urbaine, documents clearly the history of the town from the Hundred Years' War up to the present (see **BERGERAC-WHAT TO SEE**). The rue d'Albret has several old town houses and leads back again to the south end of the long rue Neuve d'Argenson. Look out for the 18thC Hôtel de Ville, once an old convent, and the Moulin des Cordeliers, a 17thC Franciscan friary mill where Bergerac's annual Festival of Art is held. The great River Dordogne is 100 m away, with the bridge leading across to Monbazillac.

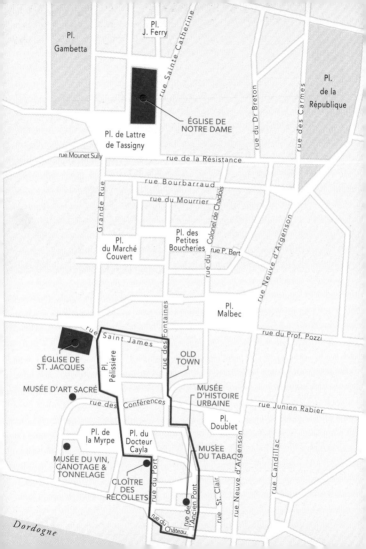

Pl. Gambetta

Pl. J. Ferry

rue Sainte Catherine

Pl. de la République

ÉGLISE DE NOTRE DAME

Pl. de Lattre de Tassigny

rue Mounet Sully

rue de la Résistance

rue du Dr Breton

rue des Carmes

rue Bourbarraud

rue du Mourrier

Grande Rue

Colonel de Chadois

Pl. du Marché Couvert

Pl. des Petites Boucheries

rue du

rue P. Bert

rue Neuve d'Argenson

Pl. Malbec

rue des Fontaines

rue du Prof. Pozzi

rue Saint James

ÉGLISE DE ST. JACQUES

Pl. Pélissière

OLD TOWN

MUSÉE D'ART SACRÉ

rue des Conférences

MUSÉE D'HISTOIRE URBAINE

rue Junien Rabier

Pl. Doublet

Pl. de la Myrpe

Pl. du Docteur Cayla

MUSÉE DU TABAC

rue Candillac

MUSÉE DU VIN, CANOTAGE & TONNELAGE

CLOÎTRE DES RÉCOLLETS

rue du Port

rue de l'Ancien Pont

rue St. Clair

rue Neuve d'Argenson

rue du Château

Dordogne

OLD TOWN
❏ 2100 Mon., Wed. & Fri., 1030 Tue. & Thu.
Tours organized by the Tourist Office from 1 July. See BERGERAC-WALK.

ÉGLISE DE NOTRE DAME Pl. de Lattre de Tassigny.
❏ 0900-1200, 1400-1700 Mon.-Sat., 0900-1200 Sun.
19thC church with several good paintings. See BERGERAC-WALK.

MUSÉE DU TABAC La Maison Peyrarède, Old Town.
❏ 1000-1200, 1400-1800 Tue.-Sat., 1430-1830 Sun. ❏ 10F.
Built in 1603, this elegant mansion houses a fascinating collection of international tobacco memorabilia. See BERGERAC-WALK.

MUSÉE D'HISTOIRE URBAINE Next to Musée du Tabac.
❏ 1000-1200, 1400-1800 Tue.-Sat., 1430-1830 Sun. ❏ 10F.
Bergerac's history, well-documented with maps, paintings, artefacts and drawings of the old Protestant centre. See BERGERAC-WALK.

CLOÎTRE DES RÉCOLLETS Maison du Vin, near Pl. Dr Cayla.
❏ 1100-1200, 1330-1730 July & Aug. ❏ 11F.
Originally cloisters housing a Protestant temple. See BERGERAC-WALK.

MUSÉE DU VIN, CANOTAGE & TONNELAGE
rue de la Myrpe, Old Town.
❏ 1000-1200, 1400-1800 Tue.-Fri., Sat. am. ❏ 10F.
Evolution of Bergerac wine growing, as well as displays on river transport (gabares) *and cooperage. See* BERGERAC-WALK.

MUSÉE D'ART SACRÉ Pl. Pélissière, Old Town.
❏ 1500-1830 Tue.-Sun. (July-Sep.). Open Sun. all year round. ❏ 9F.
Religious sculptures, paintings, vases and statues from the Middle Ages. See BERGERAC-WALK.

ÉGLISE DE ST. JACQUES Grande Rue/Pl. Pélissière.
❏ 0900-1200, 1400-1700 Mon.-Sun. am.
Pilgrim church on route to Santiago de Compostela. See BERGERAC-WALK.

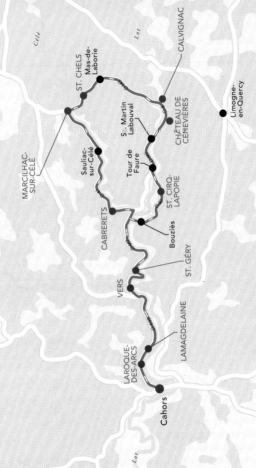

Livernon

Célé

Lot

ST. CHELS
Mas-de-Laborie

CALVIGNAC

MARCILHAC-SUR-CÉLÉ

St. Martin
Labouval

CHÂTEAU DE
CÉMEVIÈRES

Limogne-en-Quercy

Sauliac-sur-Célé

Tour de
Faure

CABRERETS

ST. CIRQ-LAPOPIE

Bouziès

ST. GÉRY

VERS

LAMAGDELAINE

LAROQUE-DES-ARCS

Cahors

Lot

Excursion 1

A one-day excursion east to the villages, chateaux and grottoes of the Lot and Célé valleys.

Leave Cahors from the northeast end following the bend of the River Lot on the D 653, initially to Laroque-des-Arcs, a village on your left. Traces of a Roman aqueduct which brought water to Cahors, and a 13th-15thC chateau can be seen. 2 km further on the Roman aqueduct passed through Lamagdelaine. Cahors wine is grown in vineyards on both sides of the river. Keep on the D 653 for 8 km to Vers, which was an English stronghold in the Hundred Years' War. On the hill overlooking the river are a grotto, a dolmen and an old paper mill. Cross over the little River Vers on the D 662, following the river loop to St. Géry, which has some fortified grottoes, and at Bouziès cross the bridge on the D 40.

35.5 km – St. Cirq-Lapopie. This must rank as the prettiest village in the Lot. Allow one hour to stroll round the score of medieval houses, church, ruined 13thC chateau and Musée Rignault (1000-1200, 1400-1800 Wed.-Mon., April-Oct.: 8F), and talk to the many artisans (wood turners, silk painters, tapestry makers, leather workers, potters, engravers and painters). There are several restaurants, including L'Atelier, Auberge du Sombral and La Pelissaria. Recross the River Lot at the east end of the village at Tour de Faure, turn right on the D 662 to St. Martin Labouval and cross the river again to see the splendid 13th-15thC Château de Cénevières (see **CHATEAUX-CAHORS & FIGEAC**). Its history dates back to the

Château du Diable

7thC Dukes of Aquitaine. Note the painted ceilings, Flemish tapestries and the alchemist's room with frescoes. Keep east on the D 8 to Calvignac where English troops held the chateau in the 13thC. Turn right and then left on the D 143, heading north for 8 km through Mas-de-Laborie to St. Chels where the English army had a watchtower with superb views over the Célé river valley to the northeast. Keep northwest on a minor road for 5 km.

62 km – Marcilhac-sur-Célé has medieval houses, the ruins of an 11thC abbey and the Grotte de Bellevue – 1.5 km north on a minor

road (1000-1200, 1400-1800 July-Oct.: 19F). The Colonne d'Hercule is one of scores of delicate columns, stalactites and stalagmites within the grotto. From Marcilhac-sur-Célé follow the river southwest for 16 km on the D 41 through Sauliac-sur-Célé.

78 km – Cabrerets. An hour is needed to look at the outside of the two castles: the 14thC Château Gontaut-Biron, and the troglodyte 12thC Château du Diable on the Rochecourbe hills above the village. The latter, the 'devil', was so called after the English freebooters who terrorized the region in the 13th-14thC. Furthermore, there is a superb grotto in the castle. The Grotte du Pech-merle (see **PREHISTORY-SITES**) is one of the most interesting in the Lot, with its Chapelle des Mammouths, Salle des Disques, signs of cave bears and drawings of bison, horses and mammoths. A combined ticket allows you to visit the Musée de la Préhistoire as well (see **PREHISTORY-MUSEUMS**, **Prehistory**). If you are exhausted by all this activity try one of Cabrerets' restaurants – La Pescalerie, La Sagne or Des Grottes. Return to Cahors on the D 41 and D 662.

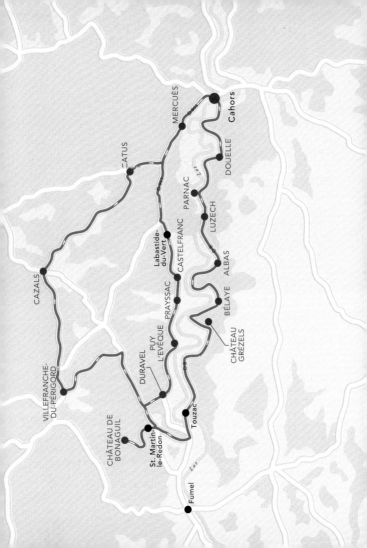

A half-day excursion west to vineyards, bastide towns (see A-Z) and chateaux.

Head northwest and west on the D 911 for 7 km to Mercuès, where there was once a temple dedicated to Mercury. The 13thC chateau, once held by the English in the Hundred Years' War, is now a top-class hotel. Continue to Labastide-du-Vert, Castelfranc (once a *bastide* owned by the bishops of Cahors) and Prayssac. Simon de Montfort (see A-Z) used this small town as a base from which to harass the Albigensians. There are good open markets and restaurants. Continue for 5 km to the west.

31 km – Puy L'Evêque was occupied by the English up to 1428, then by the Albigensians, and later by the Huguenots (see A-Z). From the top of the cliffs by La Bellevue restaurant, there is a view of the Cahors vineyards and the old river port. 6 km further on is Duravel, which has an 11thC priory church with a crypt. After Duravel turn half right through St. Martin-le-Redon and continue to the chateau of Bonaguil (see **CHATEAUX-CAHORS & FIGEAC**). This perfect 15thC military fortress is a classic folly, constructed in the wrong place (nothing to guard), and was never attacked! It is well worth a visit, especially for children. Now there are two alternatives.

Either: Go north to Villefranche-du-Périgord, a *bastide* town with good restaurants, east to Cazals, another *bastide*, and Catus, which has medieval houses and an 11thC priory, then back to Cahors.

Or: Follow the Cahors wine route along the D 8 on the south bank of the River Lot via Touzac, the 15thC chateau of Grézels (see **CHATEAUX-CAHORS & FIGEAC**), past the cliffs of Belaye, a stronghold held by English and French in the Hundred Years' War, to the pretty village of Albas, with a chateau owned by the Cahors bishops, and on to Luzech. Richard Coeur de Lion (see A-Z) took the town in 1188 and later King Philippe le Bel bartered it to the English in return for the evacuation of Cahors. There are remains of a Roman *oppidum* and 12thC keep in this town, with the River Lot on both sides. The next village, Parnac, has the region's main wine co-operative, and half a dozen wine farms at which you can taste and buy. Douelle is another pretty village beside the river before you come into the suburbs of Cahors.

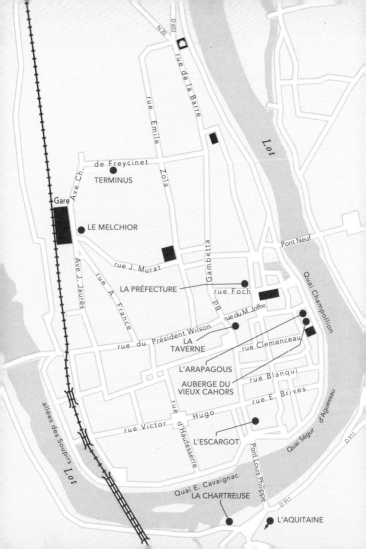

LA CHARTREUSE On south bank of river, west of Pont L. Philippe.
❏ 1200-1400, 1930-2100 Tue.-Sun. Closed Nov. ❏ Expensive.
Elegant rooms and rich cuisine; overlooking the green-blue River Lot.

TERMINUS 5 Ave Charles de Freycinet, on west side of Pl. Général de Gaulle.
❏ 1200-1400, 2000-2200 Tue.-Sun. ❏ Expensive.
Good Quercy cuisine – confit d'oie, truffled turkey – in 3-star hotel.

L'AQUITAINE Lalbenque, RN 20 dir. Toulouse.
❏ 1200-1400, 2000-2130 Tue.-Sat., 1200-1400 Mon. ❏ Expensive.
Gastronomic Quercy cuisine and Breton dishes in a 3-star hotel.

LA TAVERNE 1 rue Jean-Baptiste Delpech, off Bd Gambetta.
❏ 1200-1330, 1930-2100 Tue.-Sun. Closed Nov. ❏ Moderate.
Typical Quercy cuisine; try the pigeon rôti aux girolles.

LA PRÉFECTURE 64 rue de la Préfecture, near Cathedral.
❏ 1200-1330, 1930-2100 Tue.-Sun. ❏ Moderate.
Popular, elegant, good-value prix fixe menu; ask for gâteau aux noix.

L'ARAPAGOUS 134 rue St. Urcisse, on east side of town.
❏ 1200-1330, 1945-2115 Tue.-Sat. ❏ Moderate.
Try grillades au feu de bois or one of the regional specialities.

AUBERGE DU VIEUX CAHORS 144 rue St. Urcisse.
❏ 1200-1400, 2000-2115. ❏ Inexpensive.
The patron here is also the chef; ask for l'assiette Quercynoise.

LE MELCHIOR Pl. de la Gare.
❏ 1215-1430, 1915-2130 Mon.-Sat., 1215-1430 Sun. ❏ Inexpensive.
Good-value plat du jour, quick service, noisy and cheerful.

L'ESCARGOT 5 Bd Gambetta.
❏ 1200-1400, 1930-2045 Tue.-Sat., 1200-1400 Sun. ❏ Inexpensive.
Modestly priced three-course prix fixe menu.

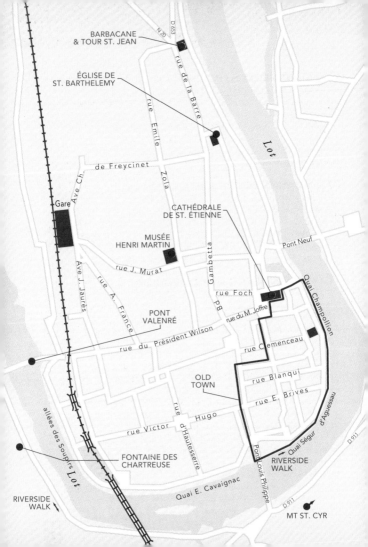

BARBACANE
& TOUR ST. JEAN

ÉGLISE DE
ST. BARTHELEMY

rue de la Barre

N 20

D 653

rue Emile Zola

Ave. Ch. de Freycinet

Gare

CATHÉDRALE
DE ST. ÉTIENNE

Lot

Pont Neuf

MUSÉE
HENRI MARTIN

rue J. Murat

Ave. J. Jaurès

rue A. France

rue Foch

Bd. Gambetta

rue du M. Joffre

Quai Champollion

PONT
VALENRÉ

rue du Président Wilson

rue Clemenceau

OLD
TOWN

rue Blanqui

rue E. Brives

rue d'Hautesserre

rue Victor Hugo

allées des Soupirs Lot

FONTAINE DES
CHARTREUSE

Quai E. Cavaignac

Pont Louis Philippe

Quai Ségur d'Aguesseau

RIVERSIDE
WALK

D 911

RIVERSIDE
WALK

MT ST. CYR

D 911

What to See

CATHÉDRALE DE ST. ETIENNE 200 m east of Bd Gambetta.
❑ 0800-1800 Mon.-Sun. am.
Built in 1154, this magnificent fortified building has three Byzantine cupolas, the chapel of St. Gausbert with frescoes, delicate Renaissance cloisters dating from 1509, and a small pilgrimage museum. Note the tympanum on the North Door, traffic notwithstanding!

OLD TOWN Between Cathedral, and south and east river banks.
Maze of medieval streets and tall 16th-17thC houses, including Maison de Roaldès where Henri IV lodged during the religious wars of 1580.

PONT VALENTRÉ
This bridge spans the River Lot to the southwest of the town. Unique in Europe, it was built in 1308 as a fortress to guard the river approaches. Take a tour (July & Aug.: times from Tourist Office) and ask about the legend of the devil and his compact with the architect of the bridge!

BARBACANE AND TOUR ST. JEAN Just off the junction of the N 20 and D 653.
14thC ramparts, guardhouse and sinister 'Tour des Pendus'.

ÉGLISE DE ST. BARTHELEMY Northeast of town between Bd Gambetta and the river.
❑ 0800-1800 Sun.
A rather ugly red brick church where Pope John XXII was baptized in 1316. Next door is the Pope's Tower, the remains of the Bishop's Palace.

MUSEE HENRI MARTIN rue Emile Zola.
❑ 1000-1230, 1500-1900 Tue.-Sun. (July & Aug.). ❑ 10F.
Housed in the original episcopal palace, with Martin's paintings of Quercy landscapes, and displays on local history and archaeology.

RIVERSIDE WALKS on Quai Ségur d'Aguessau.
East of Pont Louis Philippe, north of river, or south of river to visit the Gallo-Roman Arc de Diane and Fontaine des Chartreuse springs. Mt St. Cyr on the east bank gives superb views of the town and surroundings.

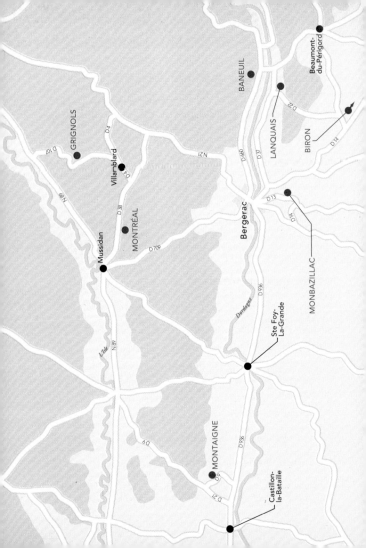

GRIGNOLS

D 104

D 4

Villamblard

D 21

MONTRÉAL

D 38

Mussidan

N 89

D 709

L'Isle

N 89

D 6

MONTAIGNE

D 9

Castillon-
la-Bataille

D 20

D 936

Ste Foy-
La-Grande

Dordogne

D 936

Bergerac

MONBAZILLAC

D 14

D 13

BANEUIL

D 21

LANQUAIS

BIRON

D 14

Beaumont-
du-Périgord

D 37

D 60

N 21

GRIGNOLS 30 km north of Bergerac on the D 107.
❑ 1400-1830 Thu.-Tue. (mid June-mid Sep.). ❑ 18F.
12th-15thC, with strong square keep on hillside as well as moats and terraces, overlooking River Vern valley.

MONTRÉAL Issac, 25 km north of Bergerac near Mussidan.
❑ 1000-1200, 1400-1800 Wed.-Mon. (July-Sep.). ❑ 18F.
Strong medieval castle on a rocky spur with ramparted towers overlooking the River Crempse.

MONTAIGNE 40 km west of Bergerac off the D 936.
❑ 0900-1200, 1400-1900 Wed.-Sun. ❑ 12F.
*The essayist Michel de Montaigne (see **A-Z**) lived and worked here. The chateau was rebuilt in 1884 in Gothic style: note especially the library.*
See **BERGERAC-EXCURSION 2**.

MONBAZILLAC 7 km due south of Bergerac.
❑ 1000-1230, 1400-1930. ❑ 16F.
*A classic grey-stoned, turreted chateau built in 1550. There are museums, wine-tasting opportunities and a good restaurant. See **BERGERAC-EXCURSIONS 1 & 2**.*

LANQUAIS 18 km east of Bergerac on the D 37.
❑ 0930-1200, 1430-1800 Fri.-Wed. (April-Oct.). ❑ 18F.
*Part medieval fortress, part Renaissance chateau, and also fully furnished, Lanquais stands on a site dominating the pretty village. See **BERGERAC-EXCURSION 1**.*

BANEUIL Lalinde, 17 km east of Bergerac off the D 660.
❑ 1400-1800 Aug. ❑ 15F.
14thC chateau built around a fortified tower.

BIRON 50 km southeast of Bergerac.
❑ Times vary; open every day exc. Tue. out of season. ❑ 25F.
*Massive fortress on a steep hill, with 12thC keep and Renaissance buildings, pavilion and chapel. See **BERGERAC-EXCURSION 1**.*

Château de Veyrignac

Château de Puymartin

BONAGUIL 50 km west of Cahors, north of the D 911.
❏ 1000-1200, 1400-1800 Mar.-Sep. (times vary out of season). ❏ 16F.
Fine example of 15thC military architecture. See **CAHORS-EXCURSION 2**.

GRÉZELS 33 km west of Cahors, south of the River Lot.
❏ 1400-1800 July & Aug. ❏ 15F.
Recently restored feudal castle of La Coste, overlooking the River Lot.
Museum of folklore and wine. See **CAHORS-EXCURSION 2**.

ROUSSILLON 10 km north of Cahors, east of the N 20.
❏ 1400-1700 Wed. & Thu. (July & Aug.). ❏ 13F.
Medieval fortress dominating the village of St. Pierre Lafeuille.

CÉNEVIÈRES 40 km east of Cahors on the D 662.
❏ 1000-1200, 1400-1800 Easter-Oct. ❏ 14F.
Medieval castle, overlooking Lot valley. 13thC keep, 16thC Renaissance
galleries, tapestries and alchemy room. See **CAHORS-EXCURSION 1**.

ASSIER 20 km northwest of Figeac on the D 653.
❏ 1000-1200, 1430-1830 Wed.-Mon. (mid June-Sep.). ❏ 16F.
Classic Renaissance chateau, beautifully restored, with remarkable fur-
nishings and facades. See **FIGEAC-EXCURSION**.

LARROQUE-TOIRAC 15 km southwest of Figeac on the D 662.
❏ 1100-1800 July-Sep. ❏ 13F.
Much damaged, much repaired 12thC fortress clinging to a hillside over-
looking the Lot valley. See **FIGEAC-EXCURSION**.

CASTELNAU Bretenoux, 12 km from St. Céré off the D 19.
❏ 0900-1200, 1400-1800 Wed.-Mon. ❏ 20F.
Red stone ramparts, 11thC keep and views. See **GOURDON-EXCURSION**.

MONTAL 3 km west of St. Céré on the D 673.
❏ 0930-1200, 1430-1800 April-Oct. ❏ 18F.
Built in 1523, destroyed by Revolutionaries, restored in 1908. Classic
style, pepper-pot roofs, near River Bave. See **GOURDON-EXCURSION**.

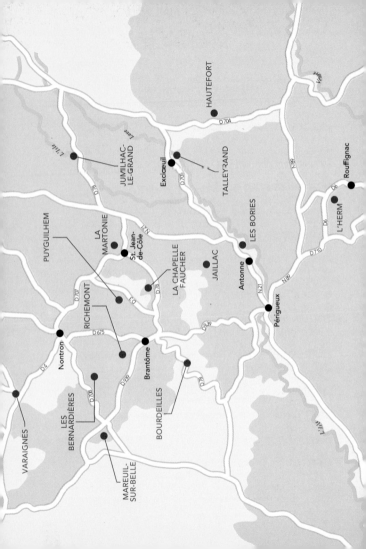

VARAIGNES Northwest of Nontron.
❏ 1000-1200, 1400-1700 Wed.-Mon. (pm only out of season). ❏ 10F.
15thC chateau housing a museum of arts and folklore.

LES BERNARDIÈRES Champeaux, southwest of Nontron.
❏ 1000-1130, 1500-1830 Wed.-Mon. (July-Sep.). ❏ 12F.
14thC keep, huge walls, dry moat: the chateau dominates the valley of the River Nizonne.

MAREUIL-SUR-BELLE 40 km northwest of Brantôme on the D 939.
❏ 1430-1830 Thu.-Tue. (July-Sep.). ❏ 12F.
A 15thC chateau with moat, drawbridge, Gothic chapel, keep, prisons and gardens.

RICHEMONT Northwest of Brantôme.
❏ 1000-1200, 1500-1800 Sat.-Thu. (mid July-Aug.). ❏ 8F.
A 16thC chateau with a solid square tower, two long wings and a deco-rated chapel with the tomb of its founder, Pierre de Bourdeille (see **Bourdeille***).*

BOURDEILLES Southwest of Brantôme.
❏ 1000-1200, 1400-1900 Wed.-Mon. ❏ 12F.
A feudal fortress enclosing a Renaissance palace overlooking the Dronne: superb views from the keep. See PÉRIGUEUX-EXCURSION 2.

LES BORIES Antonne, northeast of Périgueux on the N 21.
❏ 1000-1200, 1400-1900 July-Sep. ❏ 10F.
Built in 1497 at the end of an avenue of trees, the chateau has two round towers, a staircase and fortified exterior. It also has a Renaissance interior. See PÉRIGUEUX-EXCURSION 2.

JAILLAC 20 km northeast of Périgueux.
❏ 1430-1830 Fri.-Wed. (Easter-Sep.). ❏ 9F.
Built in the 13thC and well-restored, with many loopholes in the walls, huge rooms, chimneys and staircases. See PÉRIGUEUX-EXCURSION 2.

Hautefort

LA CHAPELLE FAUCHER 6 km east of Brantôme.
❏ 1000-1800 July & Aug. ❏ 9F.
Overlooking the River Côle, this 13th-15thC castle has two fortified towers and superb views.

PUYGUILHEM Northeast of Brantôme.
❏ 0900-1200, 1400-1900 Wed.-Mon. ❏ 25F.
Magnificent 16thC chateau with circular tower, 18thC pavilion and staircase. Well furnished and restored. See PÉRIGUEUX-EXCURSION 2.

LA MARTONIE St. Jean-de-Côle, 40 km northeast of Périgueux.
❏ 1000-1200, 1400-1900 July & Aug. ❏ 10F.
The chateau was built in the 15th-17thC and dominates the pretty village. It has two towers, a furnished wing and a monumental staircase. See PÉRIGUEUX-EXCURSION 2.

JUMILHAC-LE-GRAND 45-50 km from both Périgueux and Nontron.
❏ 1000-1200, 1400-1830 July-mid Sep. ❏ 16F.
Astonishing, beautiful, turreted Loire-style chateau overlooking the River L'Isle. Son et Lumière in season.

TALLEYRAND Excideuil, 35 km northeast of Périgueux.
❏ Closed to the public.
12thC fortress with two keeps linked by high curtain wall. Walks by River Loue around the castle. See PÉRIGUEUX-EXCURSION 3.

HAUTEFORT 45 km east of Périgueux off the D 704.
❏ 0900-1200, 1400-1800 Feb.-Nov. ❏ 18F.
Huge 17thC classic Loire-style chateau, beautifully restored, in park with terraces. See PÉRIGUEUX-EXCURSION 3.

L'HERM Rouffignac, 28 km southeast of Périgueux.
❏ 1000-1200, 1400-1830 Thu.-Tue. (July & Aug.). ❏ 10F.
16thC flamboyant Gothic-style chateau with crenellated towers, spiral staircase and bloody history. See PÉRIGUEUX-EXCURSION 1.

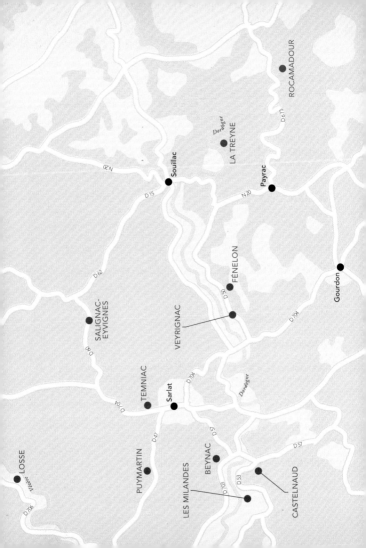

CASTELNAUD 20 km southwest of Sarlat, south of River Dordogne.
❏ 1000-1900. Closed Mon. & Sat. in winter. ❏ 20F.
*English-owned in Hundred Years' War, the chateau was built in 12thC
and dominates the rivers Céou and Dordogne: faces rival Château
Beynac. See the museum. See* **SARLAT-EXCURSION 2**.

LES MILANDES 5 km southwest of Castelnaud.
❏ 0930-1130, 1400-1830 mid Mar.-Sep. ❏ 15F.
*Made famous by Josephine Baker's orphanage, this charming
Renaissance chateau is sumptuously furnished. See* **SARLAT-EXCURSION 2**.

BEYNAC 20 km southwest of Sarlat on the D 703.
❏ 1000-1200, 1430-1830 Mar.-mid Sep. ❏ 15F.
*This immense fortress dominates the River Dordogne. Its beautifully
restored 12thC keep was once owned by Richard Coeur de Lion (see*
A-Z). *See* **SARLAT-EXCURSION 2**.

VEYRIGNAC 14 km southeast of Sarlat on the D 50.
❏ 1000-1300, 1400-1900 June-Sep. ❏ 15F.
*Feudal chateau, rebuilt in 18thC, burned by the Germans in 1944, now
well restored. See the museum of historical personages.*

FÉNELON 3 km east of Veyrignac on the D 50.
❏ 1000-1630 June-Aug. ❏ 15F.
*13th-14thC strongly fortified castle built on terraces, with two museums
and lovely views along the Dordogne valley. See* **Fénelon**.

TEMNIAC 2 km north of Sarlat off the D 704.
❏ 1000-1200, 1400-1630 Sun.-Fri., 1400-1630 Sat. (June-Sep.). ❏ 13F.
*On a romantic site, the chateau has been much damaged since the 9thC.
See the restored chapel of Notre Dame, crypt, cellars and towers.*

PUYMARTIN 11 km northwest of Sarlat on the D 47.
❏ 1000-1200, 1400-1830 June-Sep. (pm only April & May). ❏ 18F.
*Battlemented keep, 15th-16thC round towers, chapel. Well furnished,
including Aubusson tapestries. See* **SARLAT-EXCURSION 1**.

Château de Beynac

LOSSE 6 km south of Montignac on the D 706.
❑ 1000-1230, 1400-1900 June-mid Sep. ❑ 18F.
*Near Thonac, a beautiful 14th-16thC chateau overlooking the River
Vézère: sumptuously furnished. See* PÉRIGUEUX-EXCURSION 1,
SARLAT-EXCURSION 1.

SALIGNAC-EYVIGNES 20 km northeast of Sarlat on the D 60.
❑ 0900-1200, 1400-1800 Wed.-Mon. (July & Aug.); 1400-1800 Sep.-
June. ❑ 18F.
*Renovated 12thC chateau,
with ramparts, towers and
keep. See also the nearby
chateaux of St. Crepin and Le
Claud.*

ROCAMADOUR 36 km
east of Gourdon on the D 36.
❑ 0900-1200, 1330-1800
April-Oct. ❑ 6F.
Ramparts (see ROCAMADOUR-
WHAT TO SEE 1*) around
remains of 14thC fortress on
top of cliff: panoramic views.
See* GOURDON-EXCURSION,
Rocamadour.

LA TREYNE 30 km northeast of Gourdon on the D 43.
❑ 0900-1200, 1400-1800
Tue.-Sun. (June-Sep.).
❑ 12F.
*This beautiful, tranquil 17thC
chateau is now a hotel. The
park, gardens and chapel are
open to the public. See*
GOURDON-EXCURSION.

Château de Temniac

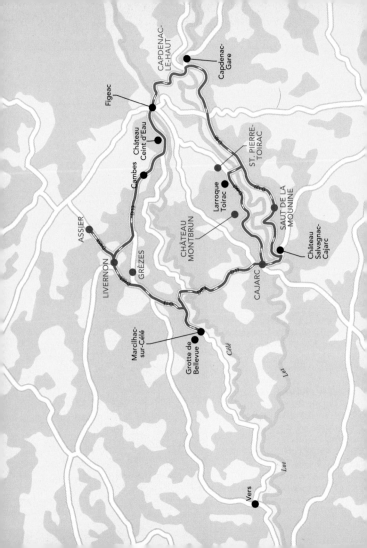

A half-day excursion to Assier, Cajarc, St. Pierre-Toirac and Capdenac.

Drive west on the D 13 past the 15thC Château Ceint d'Eau on the right (closed to the public) towards Cambes. After 5.5 km fork right on the D 113 for 4 km, then north on the D 653.

28.5 km – Assier (pop: 500). This village has two claims to fame. The two-towered Renaissance chateau with its rich furnishings (see **CHATEAUX-CAHORS & FIGEAC**) and the church, built 1540-49 with frieze, doorways and vaulting of note. Within a short distance are a dozen dolmens, curious 2000-year-old man-made stone altar-sepulchres. Retrace your route past the airport and through Livernon, occupied in 1379 by the English, to Grèzes, once a Knights Templars' stronghold (see **Knights Templars**). Keep on the D 653 for 3 km, then take the D 13 left to the River Célé. If you have not seen Marcilhac-sur-Célé and the Grotte de Bellevue (see **CAHORS-EXCURSION 1**) this is your opportunity to do so. If you have, cross the river and go southeast on the D 83 and D 17 for 14 km on pretty but winding roads.

51 km – Cajarc. President Pompidou lived here for a time. The Maison des Arts mounts contemporary exhibitions (1300-2000 April-Oct.). South of the river is the 13thC Château Salvagnac-Cajarc (closed to the public). Follow the winding river valley either on the D 662 north, or D 127 south of the river heading east, past a cliff called Saut de la Mounine or the ruined 13thC chateau of Montbrun, to Larroque-Toirac (see **CHATEAUX-CAHORS & FIGEAC**).

67 km – St. Pierre-Toirac has a fortified 11thC church. Cross the river and keep on the D 86 for 15 km.

82 km – Capdenac. The small town of Capdenac-le-Haut is on the north side of the River Lot overlooking Capdenac-Gare. Once an English stronghold, then French, then a Protestant HQ, Capdenac has rarely known peace. The 13thC keep, Musée du Donjon and Tourist Office are in the same building. The 13thC town ramparts, Gothic town gates and medieval houses of interest. Across the valley is the Fontaine Romaine at the top of a steep stairway cut in the cliff face. It is also known as Fontaine des Anglaises. Both the Musée du Donjon and Fontaine Romaine/Anglaise are open for visits (1000-1200, 1500-1900 June-Sep.: 8F each). It is 5 km to Figeac on the winding N 140.

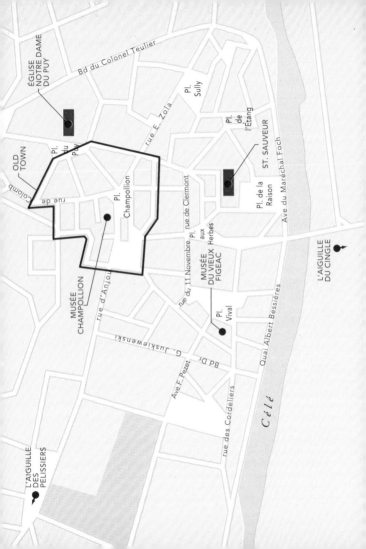

What to See

OLD TOWN

Occupied by the English in 1372, its narrow streets and 14thC buildings cover a rectangle 300 m by 400 m. Look out for Pl. Carnot, Pl. Champollion, rue de la Viguerie, rue Seguier and rue Balène. The covered passages are called arcvôlts *and the wide open-galleried lofts in some of the medieval houses are known as* solelhas.

ST. SAUVEUR (Abbey church), Pl. Michelet, 200 m east of the Tourist Office.

❏ 0900-1800 Mon.-Sun. am.
Consecrated in 1092 as a pilgrim church. The chapter room, now the chapel of Notre Dame de Pitié, is 13thC and six of the capitals are 12thC.

MUSÉE CHAMPOLLION impasse Champollion, near the Mairie.

❏ 1000-1200, 1430-1830 Easter-Sep. Closed Mon. out of season.
❏ 24F.
Jean-Francois Champollion (1790-1832), the famous Egyptologist who solved the riddle of the Rosetta stone, lived here. His life and work are commemorated, and there is a collection of art assembled from the Louvre and museums of Cahors and Rodez.

ÉGLISE NOTRE DAME DU PUY Pl. du Puy.

❏ 0900-1800 Mon.-Sun. am.
12thC Romanesque style but repaired in the 14th and 17thC.

MUSÉE DU VIEUX FIGEAC/HOTEL DE LA MONNAIE

Pl. Vival, same building as the Tourist Office.
❏ 1000-1200, 1400-1800 mid June-mid Sep. Mon.-Sat. out of season.
❏ 9F.
13thC building: lapidary collection, coins, paintings, fossils and folklore.

LES AIGUILLES (The Curious Needles)

Two of four stone needles marking land boundaries, one 14.5 m, the other 11.5 m high, outside Figeac. The Aiguille du Cingle (or Pressoir) is south on the D 922; des Pelissiers is northwest at Lissac off the D 2.

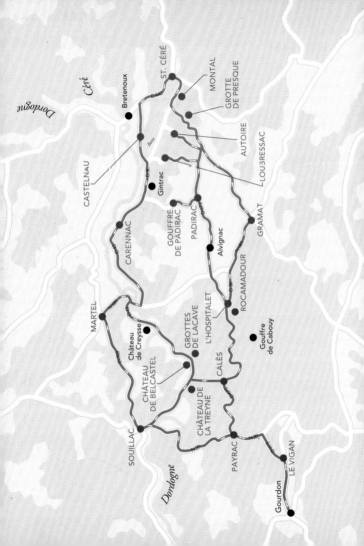

A one-day excursion to Rocamadour, Padirac and St. Céré.

Start early for this very interesting but tiring trip. Drive east on the
D 673 through Le Vigan, which has a Gothic 14thC collegiate church,
then northeast to the N 20.

13 km – Payrac. Legend has it that St. Amadour of Rocamadour
expelled the local demons and faceless ones here. Aqua Folies is a
small children's water sports park (1000-1900, mid June-mid Sep.). Go
east on the D 673 through Calès, which in the 14thC was a *bastide*
town (see **A-Z**). To the south is the Gouffre de Cabouy.

34 km – Rocamadour.

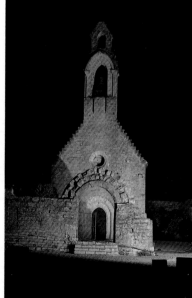

L'Hospitalet, which was once a
pilgrim hospital and then a
Knights Templars' commanderie
(see **A-Z**), now has the Forêt des
Singes (monkeys) and Grotte des
Merveilles (24,000-year-old
cave paintings). The views from
the ramparts near the fort
(closed to the public) are stunning. It is your choice whether
to park at the top of the cliffs or
drive down the hill and park in
the town of Rocamadour. Allow
one to two hours for a visit (see
CHATEAUX-SARLAT & GOURDON 2,
ROCAMADOUR-WHAT TO SEE,
Rocamadour). If you have children with you there is now a
dilemma! 3.5 km east on the
D 36 is the N 681 and 6 km to
the right and south is Gramat,
which has a large safari park of
38 ha with a variety of animals
(wild and domestic), and botani-
cal gardens (0900-2000 Easter-

Oct., 1400-1800 Nov.-Easter: 25F). The other choice is to go northeast via Alvignac to Padirac on the D 673 to see the amazing *gouffre* or chasm. The tour takes nearly two hours through a series of vast caves reached by two lifts, down to the underground river 100 m below ground, then along for 2000 m, of which 700 m is travelled by boat. It must be one of the great natural wonders of France (0900-1200, 1400-1800 April-mid Oct.: 27F). In addition, nearby is the Tropiorama Zoo (0900-2000 mid May-mid Sep.: 25F). Whichever choice you make the next stops via minor roads east of Padirac are two very pretty Quercy-style villages: Autoire, with stunning views and the Château des Anglais, and Loubressac, with a 14thC church and chateau and great panoramas, followed by the Grotte de Presque (0900-1200, 1400-1800 April-Oct.: 20F). The latter has 400 m of underground caves with curi-ously-shaped stalagmites, and is 4 km from the delightful pepper pot-roofed Montal castle, beautifully restored in 1908 (see **CHATEAUX-CAHORS & FIGEAC**). Travel 2 km east on the D 673 to the foot of the val-ley of the River Bave.

74 km – St. Céré (pop: 4500) is a good base for exploring the Auvergne to the east and the charming river valleys of the Bave, Céré and Dordogne to the north. The town boasts two museums. The Musée Jean Lurçat is on top of the hill 2 km north of the town (0930-1200, 1430-1830 mid July-Sep.: 15F). Lurçat (1892-1966) painted designs for Aubusson tapestries. The Vintage Car Museum is off the D 940, 1 km south of the town (1000-1200, 1400-1800 June-Sep.: 15F). St Céré also has a small medieval section with a score of 15th-17thC half-timbered houses, and a casino with a permanent collection of Lurçat tapestries. Keep northwest on the D 940 for 9 km.

90 km – Castelnau (3 km south of Bretenoux) is a huge feudal red stone fortress (see **CHATEAUX-CAHORS & FIGEAC**). The keep and loggia are 12thC, the ramparts 14th-15thC, the court of honour, galleries, terrace and pavilion 18thC. Beautifully restored from 1896 onwards, it is known as the second fortress of France and is a classic example of medieval military architecture. The English King Henry II fought a bloody battle here, as did Simon de Montfort (see **A-Z**) against the Albigensians in 1180. Follow the south bank of the River Céré west on the D 30 past Gintrac with its ruined chateau.

98 km – Carennac. This small village ranks among the prettiest in the region, with Fénelon's Romanesque priory-deanery, and the 12thC St. Pierre church with remarkable sculpted door and cloisters (0900-1200, 1400-1800 July-mid Sep.: 8F). The 15thC chateau, which has art exhibitions in midsummer, and the rest of the village with 16thC houses and fortified gateways, make Carennac an architectural treasure. Keep west and southwest on the D 43 to the junction with the N 681. At this point you now have a choice of routes.

Either: Go 5 km north to Martel (pop: 1500) where in 1183 Henry Curtmantel, son of King Henry II, died of fever and in disgrace. Now known as the 'Town of the Seven Towers', it has a score of medieval town houses, the 14thC church of St. Maur and two good restaurants – Le Turenne and Le Lion d'Or. Continue to the west on the D 703.

130.5 km – Souillac (pop: 4000), with its superb 12thC abbey, also has 16 hotels, several camp sites by the River Dordogne, a summer jazz festival and a curious museum of automats (1000-1200, 1500-1800, closed Mon. out of season: 15F). From Souillac take the N 20 south for 20 km, then 9.5 km west on the D 673 back to Gourdon.

Or: From Carennac stay south of the River Dordogne on the D 43 and stop off to see the 15thC Château de Creysse (closed to the public), occupied by the English in 1378.

128 km – Grottes de Lacave. The underground galleries are 1.5 km long, with lakes, stalactites and stalagmites (see **PREHISTORY-SITES**). Almost next door is the cliff-top Château de Belcastel with its 14thC keep, and a further 2 km on is the Château de la Treyne, now a hotel (see **CHATEAUX-SARLAT & GOURDON 2**). Either continue on the D 43 for 6 km to Souillac, or retrace your route and head south to Calès on the D 673 to rejoin the N 20 and D 673 back to Gourdon.

CHAPELLE DE NOTRE DAME DES NEIGES

MEDIEVAL TOWN

Bd des Martyrs

rue Jean Jaurès

Bd Cabanes

CHATEAU

ÉGLISE DES CORDELIERS

allées République

rue du Majou

ÉGLISE DE ST. PIERRE

Bd General de Genouillac

Pl. de la Libération

Bd Aristide Briande

CHAPELLE DE NOTRE-DAME DU MAJOU

GROTTE DE COUGNAC

MEDIEVAL TOWN

This stands on a rocky hill and has narrow winding streets with curious names (Majou, Zig-Zag, Tortue), surrounded by the circular roads, Ave Gambetta and Bd General de Génouillac. Look for the 13thC consul's house, now the Hôtel de Ville, the Maison du Sénéchal, and Maison d'Anglars with 14thC windows and Renaissance gateways. At the top the remains of the chateau razed by Louis XIII in 1619 give superb views of the pays de Bouriane. Local artisans practise various crafts in the town.

ÉGLISE DE ST. PIERRE Summit of old town.

❏ 0900-1200, 1400-1800 Mon.-Sun. am.
Built in 1304, it has two high towers and is fortified with machicolations and massive buttresses. It also features a 14thC west doorway, 14thC stained-glass windows and 17thC gilt carvings.

CHAPELLE DE NOTRE DAME DES NEIGES

1.5 km southeast on Ave J. Admirat.
❏ 0900-1200, 1400-1800 Mon.-Sun. am.
*14thC pilgrimage chapel with polychromatic stone 13thC Virgin and Infant, and 1698 bas-relief by Jean Tournie (see **A-Z**).*

ÉGLISE DES CORDELIERS allées République.

❏ 0900-1200, 1400-1800.
*Built in 1287 and well restored in 1971, this former monastery has an interesting 14thC font and early Gothic nave. See **Tournie**.*

CHAPELLE DE NOTRE-DAME DU MAJOU Entrance to the
old town.
❏ 0900-1200, 1400-1800 Mon.-Sun. am.
Built in 1547 on the site of an oratory near the 13thC town gates.

GROTTE DE COUGNAC 3 km north on the D 704.

❏ 0900-1100, 1400-1700 June & Sep.; 0900-1800 July & Aug. ❏ 20F.
*Two large caves – Salle des Colonnes and Salle des Peintures Préhistoriques – should be seen, particularly for the paintings of bison, deer, elephants and humans. See **Prehistory**.*

A one-day excursion southeast to Montignac and the valley of the River Vézère.

Initially travel east on the N 89 south of the river. After 4 km fork left on the D 5 to Bassilac with the airport and river on your left for 12.5 km to Le Change, which has a Romanesque church and 15thC chateau with towers. The D 45 and D 67 meander pleasantly via Montagnac d'Auberoche, Brouchaud (noted for its river fish) and Bauzens (a beautiful Romanesque church) to the first port of call.

33 km – Ajat. The village has a 12thC Romanesque church and 16thC castle with overhanging machicolated walls. 5 km southeast along the N 89 is the ruined Château de la Mouthe and a 12thC church. Travel 8 km southeast on the D 67 to Auriac-du-Périgord. The Château de la Faye is 12th-16thC, the fortified parish church is 12th-15thC and the Eco-musée de l'Abeille (bees) is open 1000-1200, 1430-1900 June-Sep.: 9F. Continue on the D 67 and turn right on the D 704.

52 km – Montignac (pop: 3200), bisected by the River Vézère, is at the northern end of prehistory country, with the Lascaux caves 2.5 km southeast (see **PREHISTORY-SITES, Lascaux**). The old priory church dates from the 14th-17thC. The Musée Eugène le Roy (see **Roy**) is mainly devoted to the author of *Jacquou le Croquant* (1000-1200, 1430-1800 closed Sun. & Jan.: 12F). From 1594 to 1642 the peasants, called *Croquants* (see **A-Z**), rose in revolt against the nobility and plundered their castles, before being crushed. Montignac has several good restaurants including Relais du Soleil d'Or, Château de Puy Robert and La Grotte. A picnic lunch on the grassy banks of the river is equally appealing. Next drive due west for 5 km on a minor road to Fanlac, with a 12thC church and 14th-17thC Château d'Auberoche. Characters from Eugène le Roy's *Jacquou le Croquant* 'lived' in Fanlac. Next go south 5 km to Thonac which has a 12thC church and 14thC Château de Losse (see **CHATEAUX-SARLAT & GOURDON 2**). Drive south 2 km on the D 65.

64 km – Sergeac. A typical old Périgord village with stone-roofed (*lauzes*) houses, the ruins of a 13thC Knights Templars (see **A-Z**) fortress and 12thC fortified church. Moreover, there are no less than five prehistoric shelters (*abris*), including Castel-Merle, discovered near Sergeac

(see **Prehistory**). 2.5 km south on the D 706 on the banks of the River Vézère is one of the prettiest villages in the region, St. Léon-sur-Vézère, with the 16thC Château de Clérans and the remarkable 12thC church with bell tower and frescoes. Le Moustier and Peyzac-le-Moustier are 5.5 km south on the D 706, with Romanesque churches and more pre-historic shelters. Now head due north on the D 6 for 5.5 km into the hills to Plazac with its pine forest, 14thC presbytery and 16thC Château de Chabans. River trout from local lakes and streams will be on the menu in the town's restaurants. Travel 4.5 km to the west.

82 km – Rouffignac. Although the village was burned by the retreating Germans in 1944, the beautiful 16thC church was spared, as were the remarkable prehistoric caves, Les Cents Mammouths. A train takes visi-tors for 4 km underground (see **PREHISTORY-SITES**). 5 km northwest on the D 31 is the Château de l'Herm (see **CHATEAUX-PÉRIGUEUX 2**). Return to Périgueux via Saint-Geyrac, with its 12thC Romanesque church, west 5 km on the D 6 to Les Versannes and 18 km northwest on the D 710 and N 89 via Niversac, St. Laurent and Boulazac, with its large 14thC chateau with great circular towers in each corner.

Excursion 2

A one-day excursion north to Brantôme, the chateau of Puyguilhem and St. Jean-de-Côle.

Leave Périgueux, past the Roman arenas, north on rue Chanzy and rue Puebla to the D 939, then west for 4 km towards Chancelade. The Augustinian Priory founded here in 1129 became an abbey and was captured by the English in the Hundred Years' War. It has a fresco of St. Thomas à Becket, and now comprises three buildings: the 12thC church, the presbytery which contains the Musée d'Art Sacré, and the conventual buildings, once the Abbot's lodgings (guided tours pm only July & Aug.: 12F). Note also the Romanesque chapel of St. Jean, and 8 km northwest on the D 1 the 12thC Priory of Merlande with notable carved capitals. Lisle is 9 km northwest on the D 1 with a 12thC church and 16thC chateau. At the Wednesday market you will find river trout, walnuts, veal and poultry. Take the D 78 northeast for 8 km through the valley of the River Dronne.

29 km – Bourdeilles. The classic medieval castle shelters a small Renaissance chateau behind its ramparts (see **CHATEAUX-PÉRIGUEUX 1**). Stay on the D 78 for 10 km.

39 km – Brantôme, known as the 'Venice of Périgord' for its rivers and canals. Its Abbey and clock tower were founded by Charlemagne in the

8thC. The local hero was the lay abbot Pierre de Bourdeille (see **A-Z**) known as Brantôme, soldier of fortune, courtier, great traveller (he went with Mary Stuart to Scotland), historian, author and ladies' man! There are many hotels and restaurants in Brantôme. Keep on the D 78 east past a large dolmen and turn onto the D 83 beside the River Dronne to Champagnac, with its 16thC church and 17thC Château de la Borie-Saulnier, and little Condat-sur-Trincou with a fine Romanesque church with buttresses and bell tower. Drive 6 km northeast on the D 3.

53 km – Villars. The splendid chateau of Puyguilhem (see **CHATEAUX - PÉRIGUEUX 2**) is 2 km north, and the Grotte de Cluzeau with its fantastic paintings is sited 3 km northeast of the town (1000-1130, 1400-1800 Wed.-Mon., Easter-Sep.: 18F). Keep driving northeast on the

Périgueux

D 82 to Milhac-de-Nontron, then southeast on the D 707.

65 km – St. Jean-de-Côle. A really stunning village with a Roman bridge, 12thC church, 18thC cloisters, small museum and Château de la Martonie (see **CHATEAUX-PÉRIGUEUX 2**). Two good restaurants overlook the village green. Next drive east on the D 707 for 7 km.

72 km – Thiviers (pop: 4200). A bustling town with 12thC church, bell tower and fortified presbytery, plus the Château de Vaucocour.

Return to Périgueux on the N 21 for 33 km, via Negrondes and Sorges, and look at the Château de Jaillac and truffle museum, which includes a short truffle hunt (see **CHATEAUX-PÉRIGUEUX 1**). On the last lap beside the River Auvézère there are several classic chateaux including Les Bories (see **CHATEAUX-PÉRIGUEUX 1**), Trigonant and Château d'Escoire.

A one-day excursion east to Excideuil and Hautefort chateaux.

Take the N 21 east out of Périgueux, through Trélissac, which has two nearby chateaux, 15thC Caussade and 18thC Septfonds, towards Sarliac-sur-L'Isle with its Romanesque church and 16thC bell tower, and 15thC Manoir de Grezignac. Keep right and follow the river, via the D 705 to Savignac-les-Églises and Coulares. Nearby are the chateaux of Conty (16thC) and La Cousse (18thC). The river divides and the D 705 now runs parallel to the River Loue for 7 km.

35 km – Excideuil (pop: 1600) withstood three efforts by Richard Coeur de Lion (see **A-Z**) to take it by storm. Besides its superb Château de Talleyrand (see **CHATEAUX-PÉRIGUEUX 2**) and 12thC Benedictine priory (Église de St. Thomas), the triangular market, cordeliers sacristy, convent and town ramparts should be seen. The town's greatest citizen,

Marshal Bugeaud, has had the main square named after him. Lunch perhaps at the Hostellerie du Fin Chapon in the Pl. du Château. Due south by a choice of two minor roads is the village of St. Raphaël, where the body of the healing St. Rémy is buried in a Romanesque church. Pilgrims still come, and there are panoramic views from the village. Drive south via the D 67.

45 km – Tourtoirac on the River Auvézère has the romantic ruins of an 11thC Benedictine Abbey. The Dordogne's greatest eccentric is buried here. Antoine Orélie de Tounens, a Périgueux lawyer (1825-78), had delusions of grandeur. He made four or five attempts, with some success, to invade and rule part of Chile (Araucania) and Patagonia as King, following in the footsteps of better-known liberators. Due east on the D 5 is Cubas-Cherveix, which has a 12thC Romanesque church and one of three curious Lanternes des Morts (the others are in Sarlat and Atur). A tall stone cylindrical tower with narrow windows, it was where corpses supposedly lay in state, but there is no access to the first floor (see **SARLAT-WALK, WHAT TO SEE**). Drive 6.5 km south on the D 704.

51.5 km – Hautefort. The majestic chateau is now once again in pristine condition after a disastrous fire in 1968 (see **CHATEAUX-PÉRIGUEUX 2**). Set in parks and gardens, with a lake on the south side and the River

Lourde to the north, this charming village in Périgord Vert deserves a visit. This is 'Ans' country. In the Middle Ages it was the most important barony of the region with villages named Ste-Eulalie-d'Ans, St. Pantaly-d'Ans, Granges-d'Ans, La Boissière d'Ans among many others. Travel 6 km southeast on the D 62.

57.5 km – Badefols d'Ans. The castle has been handsomely restored since the Germans burned it in 1944. It was owned by Bertrand de Born (1140-1215), soldier, poet and court troubadour (see **A-Z**). See also the domed 12thC church. Drive via Chatres, 4 km south on the D 62, then to St. Rabier on the D 704, and south and west on the N 89.

66 km – La Bachellerie, home of the lesser nobility (*les bas-chevaliers*). The neighbouring Château de Rastignac is a freak. It was built between 1812 and 1817 and closely resembles the American White House. Take the N 89, 29 km via Thenon, St. Pierre de Chignac and St. Marie de Chignac to Périgueux.

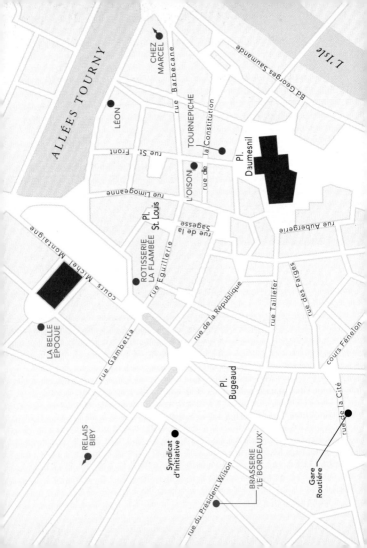

Restaurants

L'OISON (M. CHIOROZAS) 31 rue St. Front, north of Cathedral.
❑ 1200-1400, 1900-2100 Tue.-Sat., 1200-1400 Sun. Closed mid Feb.-mid Mar. ❑ Expensive.
Smart and opulent. Nouvelle cuisine; *try the* civet de lièvre *(hare).*

LÉON 18 cours Tourny, next door to Musée du Périgord.
❑ 1200-1400, 1930-2100. Closed mid May-early June & late Dec.
❑ Expensive.
Local cuisine: foie gras, cèpes, canard. *Try the Monbazillac wines.*

CHEZ MARCEL 37 Ave Limoges, 1 km on N 21, north side of river.
❑ 1200-1430, 1930-2100. Closed Tue. evening & mid July-mid Aug.
❑ Moderate.
Good-value, excellent prix fixe meals.

ROTISSERIE LA FLAMBEE 2 rue Montaigne.
❑ 1200-1400, 1900-2100 Mon.-Sat. Closed mid Dec.-mid Jan.
❑ Moderate.
Good for grills and shellfish. Ask for Pécharmant red wines.

TOURNEPICHE 2 rue Nation, 50 m north of Cathedral.
❑ 1200-1400, 1930-2100. Closed early Jan. ❑ Moderate.
18thC ambience and classic cuisine; try the vins de Bergerac.

LA BELLE ÉPOQUE 1 Pl. du Gen. Léclerc, near Palais du Justice.
❑ 1200-1400, 1900-2100 Tue.-Sun. ❑ Moderate.
Elegant setting and genuine cuisine Périgourdine.

BRASSERIE 'LE BORDEAUX' 3 rue du Président Wilson.
❑ 1130-1430, 1900-2100 Mon.-Sat. ❑ Inexpensive.
Good-value, cheerful, bustling brasserie.

RELAIS BIBY Mezarquil, 202 bis rte d'Angoulême, 2 km northwest on the N 139.
❑ 1200-1400, 1900-2030 Tue.-Sat. ❑ Inexpensive.
Typical routiers *restaurant, no frills but good food.*

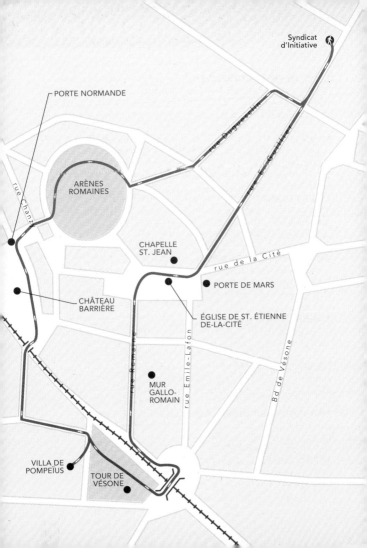

Syndicat
d'Initiative

PORTE NORMANDE

rue Duguesclin

rue du Cavillier

rue Chanz

ARÈNES
ROMAINES

CHAPELLE
ST. JEAN

rue de la Cité

PORTE DE MARS

CHÂTEAU
BARRIÈRE

ÉGLISE DE ST. ÉTIENNE
DE-LA-CITÉ

rue Romaine

rue Émile-Lafon

Bd de Vésone

MUR
GALLO-
ROMAIN

VILLA DE
POMPEÏUS

TOUR DE
VÉSONE

1 hr 30 min. *Gallo-Roman Circuit.*

Start at the Tourist Office on Ave Aquitaine. Turn right and then left onto rue Duguesclin. After 300 m is a round public garden with a fountain. You need a lot of imagination to believe that nearly 2000 years ago this Roman arena, 125 m by 153 m, held 20,000 spectators baying for blood. Large stones still identify the stairwells, vaulting area and vomitoria! About AD 275 the northern barbarians – Alemans in particular – besieged the great Roman city of Vesunna, severely damaging the main buildings. On the west side of the arena is the Porte Normande, named after a 9thC Viking siege. The massive town defence wall included a superb 3rdC Autel Taurobolique, an altar on which bulls were sacrificed, now fortunately in the Musée du Périgord (see **PÉRIGUEUX-WHAT TO SEE**). Nearby is the Maison Romane, a 12thC building with a vaulted crypt, part of the old ramparts. Next is the Château Barrière, also part of the old defences, with 12thC keep and mullioned windows. Go under the railway and south for 200 m to the rue des Vieux Cimetières, and left to see the villa built by the Gallo-Roman family of Pompeius in the 1stC AD. Look at the hypocaust, which heated the villa, and the baths, workshops and 70 sq m of mosaics (guided tours 1700 July & Aug.: 15F). Next, see the large cylindrical temple tower of Vesunna built in the 2ndC AD. It is not beautiful but is photogenic (27 m high and 20 m diameter), and stood at the centre of the forum in the largest, wealthiest and most beautiful Roman town in Aquitaine. Walk out of the gardens and turn left under the railway, and left again for 200 m on the rue Romaine to see the remains of the Gallo-Roman town walls. Keep north towards the great church of St. Etienne-de-la-Cité (see **PÉRIGUEUX-WHAT TO SEE**). This Christian sanctuary was named after a martyr (Etienne=Stephen). The two surviving cupolas date from the 11thC; inside note the 17thC altarpiece, the 12thC tomb of Bishop Jean d'Asside and the 17thC organ. The main church was badly damaged in the religious wars of the 16thC but was rebuilt in the 17thC. Opposite is the convent-chapel of St. Jean, an elegant but damaged Renaissance building (closed to the public). Just on the right the 3rdC Porte de Mars is tucked away in a private garden. Follow the rue E. Guillier for 300 m back to the Tourist Office.

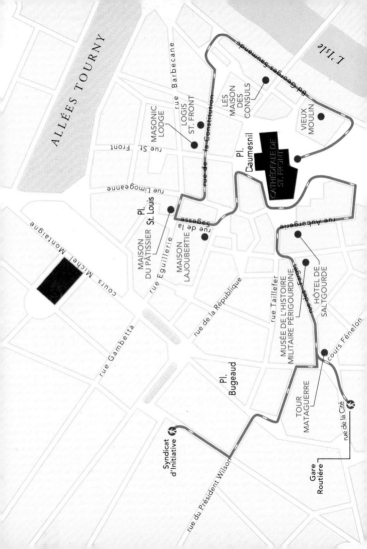

Walk 2

2 hr 30 min. *Old Town of Puy St. Front.*

Start either at the Tourist Office or at the bus station (*gare routière*) on rue de la Cité. The Tour Mataguerre (see **PÉRIGUEUX-WHAT TO SEE**), the last of 28, named after an English POW of the 15thC, was part of the defensive ramparts and stands on the corner of the rue des Farges and cours Fénelon. Look at the *hôtels* (see **A-Z**) at Nos 4 and 6. The former, Maison des Dames de la Foy, was a 17thC convent, but in 1370 was the town Governor's house (alternately French, English and French, and housed for a time the French general Du Guesclin). At No. 28 is the

Musée de l'Histoire Militaire Périgourdine, which contains World War II Resistance memorabilia among 600 years of military history (see **PÉRIGUEUX-WHAT TO SEE**). Turn right into rue Aubergerie where there are three interesting houses: No. 4, No. 8 – Hôtel de Saltgourde with 15thC tower and battlements – and No. 16 – Hôtel d'Abzac de Ladouze with two octagonal fortified towers. Follow rue St. Roch into rue du Calvaire to the cloisters and Cathédrale de St. Front (see **PÉRIGUEUX-WHAT TO SEE**). Those condemned to death in the Middle Ages passed along the 'road of Calvary' towards their execution in the Pl. de la Clautre outside the Cathedral. The rue de la Clarté is on the north side of the square. General Pierre Daumesnil, one of Napoleon's generals, was born at No. 7. The main markets are held in the Pl. du Coderc, some in the covered building,

some around the square. The Pl. de l'Hôtel de Ville has the 17thC town hall (Hôtel de Lagrange-Chancel); see also No. 7, a fortified 15thC house. Next is the rue de la Sagesse with a notable building, Maison Lajoubertie, with curious coats of arms and elegant Renaissance stairway, at No. 1 (seasonal visits arranged by Tourist Office). The Pl. St. Louis with a fountain in the centre has winter foie gras markets. On the corner of the square and rue Eguillerie is La Maison du Pâtissier or Maison Tenant, a Renaissance house with Latin inscription dating from 1518. The rue Limogeanne runs north-south and has several elegant mansions. No. 1 is Maison Lapeyre, No. 3 has King Francois I's crest of a salamander, No. 5 is the Hôtel Estignard with magnificent sculpted chimney and No. 12 is the 15thC Hôtel de Merédieu. The passage Daumesnil has a number of interesting courtyards and alleyways leading to the rue de la Miséricorde and rue de la Constitution. At No. 2 is the 15thC Hôtel Saint-Astier (Maison Ribette), No. 3 has an unusual arched doorway and No. 7 is the 15thC Logis St. Front or Hôtel de Gamançon (now the Conservation Society). Look out for the Masonic lodge in rue St. Front. The hill slopes down to the River L'Isle, and along the Bd Georges Saumande are three more *hôtels* – La Maison Lambert, 15thC Maison Cayla, also known as La Maison des Consuls, and 16thC La Maison de Lur. Keeping south you will note the Vieux Moulin, a granary that was part of the old ramparts. Walk back up towards the Cathedral.

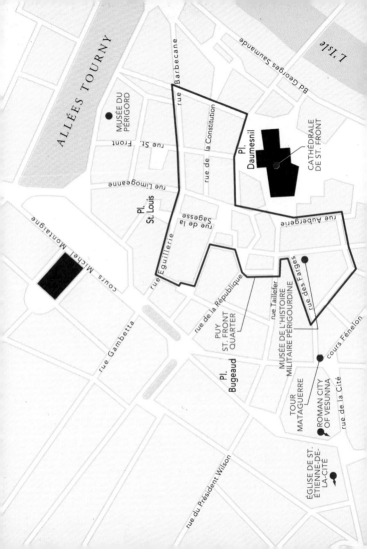

What to See

CATHÉDRALE DE ST. FRONT East side of town overlooking River L'Isle.
❏ 0800-1900. ❏ Main church free: crypt, treasury & cloisters 12F.
Partly 11thC, but restored in 19thC with amazing Byzantine cupolas and notable altarpiece; also 12thC Romanesque crypt and cloisters. See PÉRIGUEUX-WALK 2.

ROMAN CITY OF VESUNNA 500 m west of Tourist Office.
27 m-high, 2ndC tower (once a temple), Villa of Pompeius, arenas (now public gardens) and 3rdC Gallo-Roman wall. See PÉRIGUEUX-WALK 1.

MUSÉE DU PÉRIGORD allées de Tourny, 200 m north of Cathedral.
❏ 1000-1200, 1400-1800 Wed.-Mon. ❏ 10F.
A major collection of prehistory and Gallo-Roman finds, folklore, paintings and lapidary in cloisters. See PÉRIGUEUX-WALK 1.

ÉGLISE DE ST. ETIENNE-DE-LA-CITÉ North of Roman arenas.
❏ Closed Sun. pm.
Built in 12thC in Périgord-Romanesque style and rebuilt in 17thC with attractive altarpiece. See PÉRIGUEUX-WALK 1.

MUSÉE DE L'HISTOIRE MILITAIRE PERIGOURDINE
28 rue des Farges, 100 m west of Cathedral.
❏ 1000-1200, 1400-1700 Mon.-Sat. (April-Sep.). ❏ 12F.
Military history from medieval times up to the present: uniforms, flags, arms and weaponry, and paintings. See PÉRIGUEUX-WALK 2.

TOUR MATAGUERRE cours Fénelon, near bus station.
❏ Guided tours 1430 Tue.-Fri. (July & Aug.). ❏ 15F.
15thC tower with parapet. See PÉRIGUEUX-WALK 2.

PUY ST. FRONT QUARTER North and west of Cathedral.
Recently renovated area of 15thC town mansions and hôtels (see **A-Z***) with courtyards, staircases and elegant Renaissance facades. Mostly pedestrianized. See* PÉRIGUEUX-WALK 2.

LES EYZIES-DE-TAYAC Musée National de la Préhistoire, Ave du Château.
❏ 0930-1200, 1400-1800 Wed.-Mon. ❏ 15F (half price Sun.).
In 13thC fortress built into cliffs overlooking the town. See **SARLAT-EXCURSION 1, Les Eyzies-de-Tayac.**

PÉRIGUEUX Musée du Périgord, allées de Tourny.
❏ 1000-1200, 1400-1800 Wed.-Mon. ❏ 10F.
One of the most important prehistory museums in France. See **PÉRIGUEUX-WALK 1, WHAT TO SEE.**

LE THOT 2 km north of Thonac.
❏ 0930-1900 July & Aug. Reduced times and closed Mon. out of season. ❏ Combined ticket with Lascaux II 40F.
Centre of prehistory southwest of Montignac. See **PREHISTORY-SITES, Lascaux.**

BRANTÔME Musée Desmoulin/Préhistoire, Ave Fernand-Desmoulin, in the former abbey, north of the town.
❏ 1000-1200, 1400-1800 Wed.-Mon. (April-Sep.). ❏ 5F.
A collection of prehistoric art, shared with the Desmoulin's paintings.

EYMET Musée de la Préhistoire, in chateau.
❏ 1000-1200, 1500-1900 Mon.-Sat., 1500-1900 Sun. (mid June-mid Sep.). Out of season pm only. ❏ 10F.
An exhibition of local prehistory finds, as well as folklore traditions.

PEYZAC-LE-MOUSTIER Musée de la Préhistoire, 9 km northeast of Les Eyzies-de-Tayac.
❏ 0900-1830 July & Aug. ❏ 8F.
Many fossils and flint instruments are on view.

CABRERETS Musée de la Préhistoire, on the D 41 33 km east of Cahors.
❏ 0930-1200, 1330-1730 April-Oct. ❏ Museum & site 32F.
An exhibition of dig finds. See **CAHORS-EXCURSION 1, PREHISTORY-SITES.**

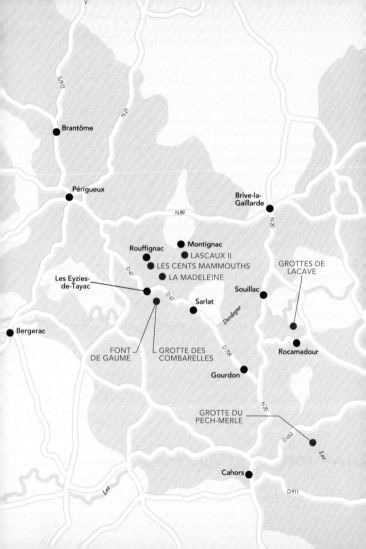

FONT DE GAUME 2 km east of Les Eyzies-de-Tayac on the D 47.
❏ 0900-1200, 1400-1800 Wed.-Mon. ❏ 25F.
Paintings of horses, deer and bison. See **SARLAT-EXCURSION 1.**

GROTTE DES COMBARELLES 3 km east of Les Eyzies-de-Tayac.
❏ 0900-1200, 1400-1800 Wed.-Mon. ❏ 25F.
Hundreds of engravings of animals and, unusually, of men. See **SARLAT-EXCURSION 1.**

LES CENTS MAMMOUTHS Rouffignac, 14 km north of Les
Eyzies-de-Tayac on the D 47 and D 32.
❏ 0900-1130, 1400-1800. ❏ 25F.
4 km via underground electric train to see fine paintings of mammoths, horses and bison. See **PÉRIGUEUX-EXCURSION 1.**

LASCAUX II 2.5 km southeast of Montignac.
❏ 0930-1900 July & Aug.; 1000-1200, 1400-1700 Wed.-Mon. (Sep.-June). ❏ Combined ticket with Le Thot 40F.
Amazing modern replica of the famous caves. See **PREHISTORY-MUSEUMS, Lascaux**.

LA MADELEINE Tursac, 8 km northeast of Les Eyzies-de-Tayac.
❏ 0900-1200, 1400-1900 July & Aug.; 1000-1200, 1400-1700 Wed.-Mon. (Sep.-June). ❏ 20F.
Troglodyte village of prehistoric man.

GROTTES DE LACAVE 10 km from both Rocamadour and
Souillac, on River Dordogne.
❏ 0900-1200, 1400-1800 April-mid Oct. ❏ 25F.
Electric train to a series of huge caves, with prehistoric weapons, lakes and stalactites. See **GOURDON-EXCURSION**.

GROTTE DU PECH-MERLE Cabrerets, 33 km east of Cahors.
❏ 0930-1200, 1330-1730 April-Oct. ❏ Site & museum 32F.
Excellent variety of paintings and engravings, including mammoths, horses and a bear. See **CAHORS-EXCURSION 1, PREHISTORY-MUSEUMS.**

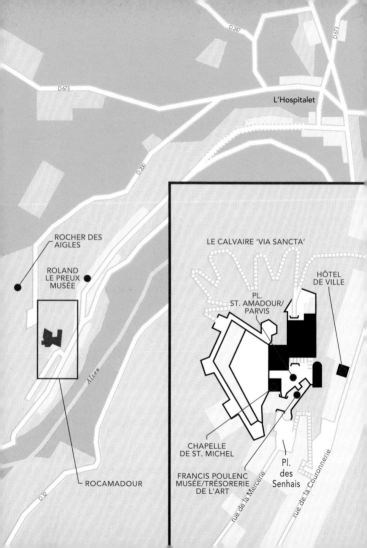

D 247

D 673

D 673

L'Hospitalet

D 673

D 20

ROCHER DES
AIGLES

ROLAND
LE PREUX
MUSÉE

Alzou

ROCAMADOUR

D 32

LE CALVAIRE 'VIA SANCTA'

HÔTEL
DE VILLE

PL.
ST. AMADOUR/
PARVIS

CHAPELLE
DE ST. MICHEL

FRANCIS POULENC
MUSÉE/TRÉSORERIE
DE L'ART

rue de la Mercerie

Pl.
des
Senhais

rue de la Couronnerie

PLACE ST. AMADOUR/PARVIS

A group of seven churches or chapels including 11th-13thC Basilica of St. Sauveur, with a crypt below, the chapel of Notre Dame, with the famous Black Madonna, a 'miraculous' bell and, outside, Roland's famous sword Durandel, thrust into the cliff face.

HOTEL DE VILLE rue de la Couronnerie.
❑ 1000-1200, 1400-1800 Thu.-Tue. (May-Sep.). ❑ 5F.
Built in the 15thC, it has some fine Jean Lurcat tapestries. Also see the Figuier, Fort and Saumon gateways.

CHAPELLE DE ST. MICHEL On rock face, next to Francis Poulenc Musée.
12thC frescoes and a chancel.

FRANCIS POULENC MUSÉE/TRÉSORERIE DE L'ART SACRÉ Pl. St. Amadour/Parvis.
❑ 0900-1200, 1400-1800 April-Nov. ❑ 10F.
Reliquaries, monstrance, caskets and crosses in silver and gold from various sanctuaries.

ROLAND LE PREUX MUSÉE rue de la Couronnerie.
❑ 0900-1200, 1400-1900 July-Sep. ❑ 15F.
The history of Rocamadour and pilgrimages portrayed in wax.

LE CALVAIRE 'VIA SANCTA'
Stations of the Cross on a winding path with 223 steps up the cliff side from Rocamadour to L'Hospitalet.

CASTLE RAMPARTS On top of cliff.
❑ 0900-1200, 1330-1800 April-Oct. ❑ 6.50F.
14thC ramparts with superb panoramas over Rocamadour.

ROCHER DES AIGLES On top of the cliffs west of L'Hospitalet.
❑ 1000-1900 Easter-mid Nov. ❑ 18F.
Guided tours to see eagles, flying displays and breeding grounds.

D 247

D 673

GROTTE
DES
MERVEILLES

L'Hospitalet

FORET DES SINGES

D 673

JARDIN
DES PAPILLONS

D 673

D 200

Rocamadour

Alzou

D 32

GROTTE DES MERVEILLES 250 m north of L'Hospitalet, off the D 673.
❏ 1000-1200, 1400-1800 April-Oct. ❏ 15F.
Cave paintings, limestone dams, stalactites and stalagmites.

JARDIN DES PAPILLONS L'Hospitalet.
❏ 1000-1200, 1400-1800 May-mid Oct. ❏ 22F.
Butterfly sanctuary.

FORET DES SINGES East of L'Hospitalet off the D 36.
❏ 1000-1200, 1400-1800 April-mid Nov. ❏ 10F.
150 Barbary apes in surroundings resembling their natural habitat.

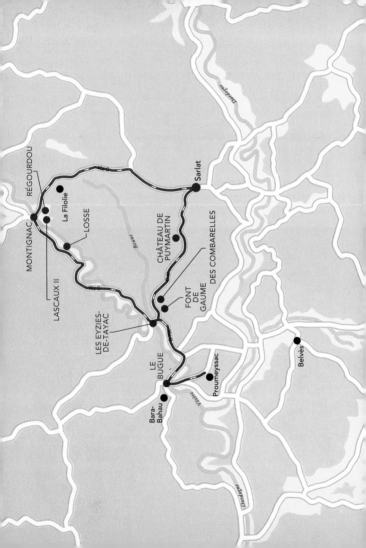

A one-day excursion northwest to chateaux, grottoes and prehistoric caves.

Head north on the D 6 and west on the D 47 for 8 km to the 15thC Château de Puymartin on the right, with towers, fortified wall, Flemish tapestries and 18thC paintings (see **CHATEAUX-SARLAT & GOURDON 1**). The D 47 then continues parallel to the little River Beune to two well-known grottoes, Des Combarelles and Font de Gaume (see **PREHISTORY-SITES**).

22 km – Les Eyzies-de-Tayac (see **PREHISTORY-MUSEUMS**, **SITES**, **A-Z**, **Prehistory**). This little town (pop: 900) is the centre for Périgord prehistory on the River Vézère, and is also a tourist trap in midsummer. There is plenty to see: the Musée National de la Préhistoire is in the castle clinging to the cliff face (outside is the large curious statue of *L'Homme Primitif*) and the Musée de Spéléologie (pot-holing) is 1 km on the rte de Périgueux. Also look at the Herbarium and the 10thC fortified church. Lunch perhaps, at either the Laugerie Basse or Mentalo restaurants. Ask at the Tourist Office for the leaflet *Au Pays des Grottes* which clearly identifies 26 local grottoes, *abris* (prehistoric shelters), monuments and museums. The town of Le Bugue is 7 km southwest on the D 706, a market town (pop: 3000) with two interesting caves nearby, Bara-Bahau and Proumeyssac. But the river valley 24 km northeast to Montignac is far more attractive with many interesting caves and grottoes, troglodyte villages, several chateaux – two of which are Clerans . (closed to the public) and Losse (see **CHATEAUX-SARLAT & GOURDON 2**), which was once owned by a Scottish captain of the King's Guards – and marvellous views at every bend of the river.

46 km – Montignac is where the Grotto Lascaux II should be seen, the brilliant modern replica of the original unique cave (see **PREHISTORY-SITES**, **Lascaux**). Nearby is the Régourdou site where the 70,000-year-old skeleton of a man was discovered, which can now be seen in the Musée du Périgord in Périgueux (see **PREHISTORY-MUSEUMS**). Head east and southeast on the D 704 back to Sarlat. On the 25 km journey look at the chateau of La Filolie (closed to the public) on the right-hand side, 5 km from Montignac.

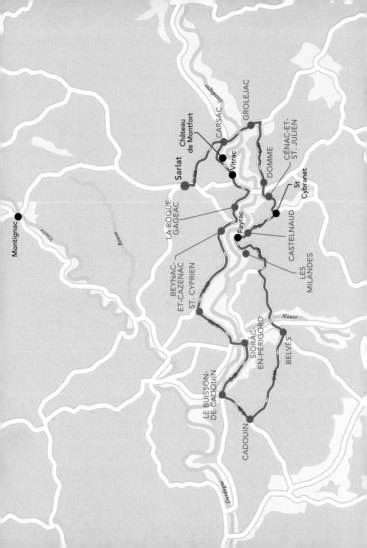

Excursion 2

A one-day excursion west and southwest to bastide *towns (see* **A-Z**),
abbeys and chateaux.

Travel south on the D 704 for 8 km to Carsac, with a delightful 15thC
church, and cross the River Dordogne to Grolejac, with good swimming, a camp site and hotels, then west on the D 50.
23 km – Domme is an interesting little *bastide* town, founded in 1280,
perched on a hill with superb views, ramparts, covered market and
public gardens. Inside the market is the entrance to 400 m of grottoes
(1000-1200, 1500-1800 Easter-Oct.: 18F), and nearby is the Paul
Reclus folklore museum (1000-1200, 1500-1800 Easter-Sep.: 11F). The
Tourist Office, in Pl. de la Halle, organizes guided visits to the *bastide*
part of the town to see the watchtowers and sinister oubliettes. There

are two good restaurants, L'Esplanade and Relais du Chevalier, both moderately priced. Cénac-et-St. Julien, at the foot of the hill, has good camp sites and swimming and two Romanesque churches. Keep heading west on the D 50 via St. Cybranet and north for 4 km on the D 57 to see a fine cluster of castles – Castelnaud (see **CHATEAUX-SARLAT & GOURDON 1**), Fayrac (closed to the public) and Les Milandes (see **CHATEAUX-SARLAT & GOURDON 1**). Take the D 53 southwest for 10 km.

40 km – Belvès (pop: 1600) is a medieval town with seven towers on the skyline, overlooking the River Nauze. Stroll round the central Pl. d'Armes to see the 15thC market hall, a chateau with a 12thC keep, a 15thC belfry, and several medieval and Renaissance houses. Head 12 km west along the D 54.

52 km – Cadouin has a Cistercian abbey and cloisters built in 1115, which housed a holy shroud (comparable to that of Turin). Many kings including Richard Coeur de Lion (see **A-Z**), St. Louis and Charles V of France came here on pilgrimage to kneel before the shroud. In 1934 experts decreed that it was not genuine and pilgrimages were discon-

tinued. A small pilgrimage museum is in the chapterhouse (guided tours 0900-1200, 1400-1900 Feb.-mid Dec., closed Tue. out of season: 12.50F). Go north on the D 25 for 6 km.

58 km – Le Buisson-de-Cadouin has camp sites and good swimming. Follow the river east on the D 25 to Siorac-en-Périgord, which is a tourist centre with four hotels and restaurants, a 17thC chateau (now the *mairie*) and small Romanesque church. Cross the River Dordogne and drive east on the D 703.

74 km – St. Cyprien (pop: 1900) has a large 12thC abbey with belfry, keep and luxurious 17thC furnishings. The D 703 continues on the north side of the river. Stop at Beynac-et-Cazenac for an hour to visit the fortress once captured by Richard Coeur de Lion (see **A-Z**), later destroyed by Simon de Montfort (see **A-Z**), but thankfully now beautifully restored (see **CHATEAUX-SARLAT & GOURDON 1**). Follow the D 703 and get another view of the fine castles on the south bank of the river.

95 km – La Roque-Gageac is an attractive village huddling under the cliffs, with 12thC Château de la Malartrie and superb views of the Dordogne valley. There are several good, moderate to expensive restaurants here, and boat cruises are available (see **Boat Trips**). Go through Vitrac on the D 703 to see the outside of the much-restored Château de Montfort, in a delightful setting (closed to the public). It is then 8 km north back to Sarlat.

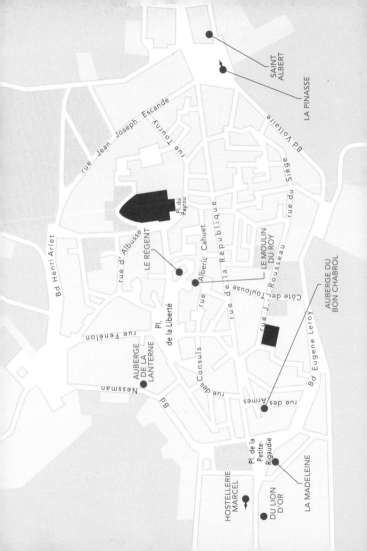

SAINT ALBERT

LA PINASSE

Bd Voltaire

rue Jean Joseph Escande

rue Tourny

rue du Siège

Bd Henri Arlet

Pl. du Payrou

rue d'Albusse

LE RÉGENT

rue Albéric Cahuet

rue de la République

LE MOULIN DU ROY

rue du Roy

Côte de Toulouse

rue Jean-J. Rousseau

AUBERGE DU BON CHABROL

rue Fénelon

Pl. de la Liberté

Bd Nessman

AUBERGE DE LA LANTERNE

rue des Consuls

rue des Armes

Bd Eugène Leroy

Pl. de la Petite-Rigaudie

LA MADELEINE

HOSTELLERIE MARCEL

DU LION D'OR

Restaurants

LA MADELEINE 1 Pl. de la Petite-Rigaudie.
❑ 1200-1400, 2000-2130. Closed Jan.-mid Mar. ❑ Expensive.
Haute cuisine – ask for gâteau au Monbazillac – and private terrace.

AUBERGE DE LA LANTERNE 18 Bd Nessmann.
❑ 1200-1400, 1930-2100 Sat.-Wed. ❑ Moderate.
Specialities are river fish, confits d'oie, liver pâté and foie gras.

LE MOULIN DU ROY rue A. Cahuet/passage H. de Ségogne.
❑ 1200-1400, 1930-2200. Closed mid Nov.-mid Mar. ❑ Moderate.
In old restored mill house: modestly priced menus and wines.

SAINT ALBERT Pl. Pasteur, near PTT (post office).
❑ 1200-1400, 1945-2100 Mon.-Sat., 1200-1400 Sun. ❑ Moderate.
Sarlat's oldest family-run hotel. Try filet de brochet braisé au Pécharmant.

LA PINASSE Le Pontet, near SNCF.
❑ 1200-1400, 2000-2100. Closed Jan. ❑ Moderate.
Shellfish and river fish dishes only. Terrace for summer meals.

LE RÉGENT 6 Pl. de la Liberté, near Tourist Office.
❑ 1130-2100. Closed Jan. & Feb. ❑ Moderate.
Serves cuisine Périgourdine and fish dishes. Brasserie open all day.

HOSTELLERIE MARCEL 8 Ave de Selvès.
❑ 1200-1400, 1900-2030 Tue.-Sun. Closed mid Nov.-mid Feb.
❑ Inexpensive.
Popular, good prix fixe menus; try poulet basquaise.

AUBERGE DU BON CHABROL 2 rue des Armes.
❑ 1200-1400, 1900-2100. ❑ Inexpensive.
Old hôtel particulier: authentic rich Périgordin cuisine. Terrace outside.

DU LION D'OR 48 Ave Gambetta, near Centre Culturel.
❑ 1200-1400, 2000-2130. Closed Dec.-April. ❑ Inexpensive.
Good-value prix fixe menus and local wines.

TOUR DU
BOURREAU

Bd Voltaire

TOUR DU GUET

rue Jean Joseph Escande

rue Tourny

rue des Fontaines

Cour du Payrou

Pl. du Payrou

CATHÉDRALE
ST-SACERDOS

ABBAYE
STE-CLAIRE

rue Albéric Cahuet

André Malraux

rue Montaigne

rue Albéric Cahuet

rue de la République

Côte de Toulouse

rue d'Albusse

rue Landry

LANTERNE DES
MORTS

PRÉSIDIAL

Bd Henri Arlet

rue de la Sélgmadre

MUSÉE
D'ART SACRÉ

Bd Eugène Leroy

Pl. de la
Liberté

rue des Consuls

ÉGLISE DE
STE-MARIE

rue Fénelon

Bd Nessman

rue Jean Jacques Rousseau

Pl. de la
Petite-
Rigaudie

2 hr.

Start from the Tourist Office in the Pl. de la Liberté. Turn sharp right through the passage Henri de Ségogne and impasse des Violettes to Pl. André Malraux. You may have already noticed half a dozen *hôtels* (see **A-Z**), some dating from the 13thC. The 16thC Maleville has been acquired by the Tourist Office; the Dautrerie and Royère (a pharmacy now) are also 16thC. The gorgeous Renaissance Hôtel de la Boétie was built in 1525 with mullioned windows and gabled roof. In the Pl. du Payrou the huge 12th-14thC Cathédrale St. Sacerdos is facing you (see **SARLAT-WHAT TO SEE**). Inside look at the fine altars, 16thC choirstalls and 18thC organ. Next door is the Italianate Renaissance Bishop's Palace (now the theatre). Keep south along the rue Tourny for 50 m and turn left into the cour des Fontaines. Inside on the left are the cloisters, the 17thC chapel of the Pénitents Bleus monks and the cour des Chanoines. Keep bearing left round the east side of the Cathedral and immediately on your right on the slope is the unusual Lanterne des Morts, also known as the Tour St. Bernard (see **SARLAT-WHAT TO SEE**). This curious 12thC monument stands in the Jardin des Enfeus and is one of three similar structures in the Dordogne. Cross over the rue Montaigne into the rue d'Albusse and round the corner on your right is the Présidial, where King Henri II dispensed his royal justice in 1552 (see **SARLAT-WHAT TO SEE**). Descend the rue Landry and rue de la Salamandre, which has several *hôtels*, for instance the 15thC Génis and Grézel, towards the Hôtel de Ville on the east side of the Pl. de la Liberté. You may also have noticed a number of handsome stone *escaliers* (staircases) in Sarlat's narrow streets as well as some old street fountains.

Bear half right past the church of Ste-Marie and just past it on the right is the large 15thC chateau, and the *hôtels* of Gisson, Vassal and Magnanat. Ahead is the rue des Consuls with, on the left, the cloth merchants' guild house, partly 14thC, called Hôtel Plamon or Maison des Consuls. Look out for two more town *hôtels*, Mirandol and Tapinois de Betou – both 15thC – and, tucked away, the Fontaine Ste-Marie. On the left is the Pl. des Oies, where the Saturday goose and foie gras markets are held. Keep straight ahead, across the busy 'Traverse', as the rue de la République is called (see **SARLAT-WHAT TO SEE**), into the narrow rue

des Armes. There are some half-timbered houses (*maisons à colombages*) and several town gateways, including Nord and L'Endrevie. At the end turn left on the Bd Eugène Leroy and take the second left, rue de la Charité, leading to the 17thC Chapelle des Pénitents Blancs, which houses the Musée d'Art Sacré (see **SARLAT-WHAT TO SEE**). Keep south on the rue J.-J. Rousseau for 100 m to where the huge 17thC Abbaye Ste-Claire and cloister are being restored. Beyond it in the rue du Siège, there are remains of the old ramparts including, on the left, the Tour du Guet (watchtower), and on the right the Tour du Bourreau (execution tower). From the watch-tower in the rue Rousset it is 100 m to the 'Traverse' and 200 m to the Cathedral.

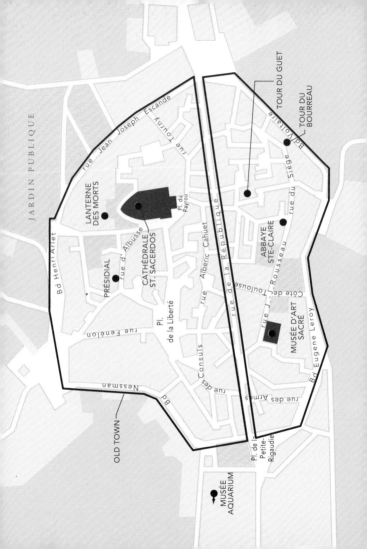

What to See

OLD TOWN East of the rue de la République.
Beautifully restored since 1964. A score of medieval town hôtels (see
A-Z*) with courtyards, fountains and heavy stone roofs (lauzes). Perhaps*
the most attractive town in the Dordogne. See **SARLAT-WALK***.*

CATHÉDRALE ST. SACERDOS In the Old Town.
❏ 0800-1800.
Built in 12th-14thC, and rebuilt in 16th-17thC with a Romanesque west
facade, tower and belfry, it also has a sacristy of 1320 and vaulted nave
of 1683. The organ was designed in 1770. See **SARLAT-WALK***.*

PRESIDIAL rue d'Albusse.
The Palais de Justice built by King Henri II in 1552. A dignified building
with a large garden overlooking the Old Town. See **SARLAT-WALK***.*

LANTERNE DES MORTS East of the Cathedral.
A conical stone tower built in 1180 to commemorate St. Bernard's ser-
mons to the faithful of Sarlat in August 1147. No one is absolutely sure
of its original purpose. See **SARLAT-WALK***.*

MUSÉE D'ART SACRÉ rue J.-J. Rousseau.
❏ 1000-1200, 1500-1800 exc. Sun. am (Easter-end Oct.). ❏ 10F.
16th-18thC statues, baroque retables, pièta, etc. See **SARLAT-WALK***.*

MUSÉE AQUARIUM rue du Commandant Maratuel.
❏ 1000-1200, 1430-1800; 1000-1900, mid June-mid Sep. ❏ 18F.
Thirty species of river fish in aquarium. Museum has exhibits on water-
related activities such as fishing, fishermen, netting, etc.

RUE DE LA RÉPUBLIQUE ('TRAVERSE') West side.
Two watchtowers, 17thC Abbaye Ste-Claire, and narrow alleys and
streets, some of which are being restored. See **SARLAT-WALK***.*

JARDIN PUBLIQUE
Dates from 17thC when it was the private garden of the bishops of
Sarlat. Large peaceful area called Jardin du Plantier.

Accidents & Breakdowns: Motorists involved in a traffic accident must complete a *constat à l'amiable* before the vehicle is moved. If the vehicle has been seriously damaged, an expert's examination is advisable prior to your return to the UK. The *constat à l'amiable* was introduced by the French insurance companies and represents the European Accident Statement Form. It must be signed by the other party, but if a dispute arises and one of the parties involved should refuse to complete the *constat à l'amiable*, then the other party should immediately obtain a written report from a bailiff (*huissier*), which is known as a *constat d'huissier*. A bailiff can usually be found in any large town and charges a fee of 400F for preparing the report. Normally the police are only called out to accidents when persons are injured, a driver is under the influence of alcohol, or the accident impedes traffic flow. If your vehicle breaks down obtain local assistance as there is no countrywide motoring club road service in France. For assistance on a motorway, telephone the *brigade de gendarmerie* from an emergency telephone or service station. The police will contact a garage for you, but should it be necessary to remove the vehicle from the motorway for repair, the choice of repair garage can be determined by the motorist. For AA members there is an emergency service, tel: 05302222 or 21872121. For RAC members, tel: 21963530, and for motorists covered by a Europ Assistance policy, tel: 19-4416801234. The AA has a port service in Calais, Boulogne and Cherbourg. See **Consulates**, **Driving**, **Emergency Numbers**.

Accommodation: Hotels – there are five categories: * (basic), ** (comfortable), *** (very comfortable), **** (high class) and ***** (luxury). A double room costs anything between 150F and 1500F a night. The cheaper, more basic hotels are usually near the rail and bus stations. You will find booking facilities at the main Tourist Offices in each town. They offer help with last-minute difficulties, but not necessarily the best deal. The Auberge de Jeunesse in each main town offers economic lodgings. Modest bed and breakfast lodgings at farmsteads, called *fermes auberges, gîtes ruraux* or *chambres d'hôtes,* often offer interesting, inexpensive alternatives to either hotels or camp sites. You can often negotiate for an evening meal with the family. Details from

all Tourist Offices or Assoc. des Gîtes du Quercy, Maison de l'Agriculture, 53 rue Bourseul, 46003 Cahors, tel: 65223283 or Assoc. de Tourisme Rural, 430 Ave Jean Jaurès, 46003 Cahors. In the Dordogne both offices are at 16 rue du President Wilson, 24009 Périgueux, tel: 53534435. See **Camping & Caravanning**, **Holiday Villages**, **Roulotte à Cheval**, **Tourist Information**, **Youth Hostels**.

Airports:

Périgueux-Bassilac	tel: 53544119.
Bergerac-Roumanière	tel: 53573136.
Sarlat-Domme	tel: 53283295.
Cahors-Lalbenque	charter flights only, tel: 65210048.
Figeac-Livernon	tel: 65405704.

These are minor regional airports used by French domestic airlines based in Paris, Bordeaux and Toulouse.

Banks: See **Currency**, **Money**, **Opening Times**.

Bastide Towns: In the mid-13thC the English and French rulers of Aquitaine decided to build new towns – *villeneuves* or *bastides* – for commercial and military reasons. Both English and French architects used the same arrangement of a rectangular gridiron sited near a main road or river, usually 440 m long and 240 m wide, with fortified walls, six fortified gateways and always a large strongly fortified church and covered market in the main square. Three main streets ran north to south bisected by many narrower streets running east to west, called *ruelles* or *carreyrons*. A moat would surround the little town, which provided shelter for several thousand inhabitants. Nearly 150 *bastides* were built on the Anglo-French frontiers between 1250 and 1350, mostly by the English. Twenty-three still survive in one form or another. The best preserved in the Dordogne are Monpazier (see **BERGERAC-EXCURSION 1**), Domme (see **SARLAT-EXCURSION 2**) and Eymet (see **BERGERAC-EXCURSION 1**); and in the Lot, Lauzerte, Castelnau-Montratier and Beauregard.

Bergerac: Pop: 28,000. The second town in the Dordogne department. Built mainly on the north side of the river, it is surrounded by vineyards and fields of tobacco – both of which it is famous for. The old town has now been restored and pedestrianized. With three museums, a summer season of jazz concerts and folklore exhibitions, Bergerac is an up-and-coming tourist centre with excellent wine and *bastide* tours and river boat cruises. There are 14 hotels and the many restaurants often have freshwater fish dishes. See **BERGERAC**, **Boat Trips**, **Events**, **Tourist Information**.

Best Buys: Local food and wine. See **Shopping**, **Wines**.

Bicycle & Motorcycle Hire: The good roads make cycling a sensible way to see the sights.

Périgueux	Au Tour de France, 96 Ave du Maréchal Juin, tel: 53534191.
	Huot Sports, 41 bis cours St. Georges, tel: 53533156.
Bergerac	Mazeau, 11 Pl. Gambetta, tel: 53570719.
	Marcel Seurin, 114 Bd de l'Entrepôt, tel: 53577199.
Sarlat	Au Vélo Dingo, Pl. André Malraux, tel: 53310093.
	Garage Matigot, 52 Ave Gambetta, tel: 53590360.
Cahors	Combes, 117 Bd Gambetta, tel: 65350673.
Les Eyzies	SNCF or Tourist Office, tel: 53069705.
Riberac	S. Lissandreau, 85 rue du 26 Mars 1944, tel: 53901630.
Souillac	Au Vélo Dingo, rue de Paliès, tel: 53310093.
	SNCF, tel: 65327821.

Some SNCF stations (as above plus Sarlat, Bergerac, Belvès, Lalinde and Cahors) will rent you a bicycle, if you leave a deposit and proof of identity and a local address. Rental averages 30-40F per day (160-180F per week) and there is a deposit of 250-300F.

Boat Trips: Many boat cruises are available on the rivers Dordogne and Lot. The round trips take about 1 hr and cost 35F (less for children and groups). Gabares de Beynac and St. Martial de Nabirat (10 km southwest of Sarlat) offer trips 1000-1900 May-Oct. There are also 1- to 2-hr trips from Bergerac, tel: 53570231, and Les Norbert at La Roque-Gageac, tel: 53294044, which cover 7.5 km and pass five castles: 40F. On the River Lot two companies offer river boat cruises: Les Bateaux Safaraid at Bouziès, tel: 65362354, and at Cahors, tel: 53667443. These are day- or half-day tours. Further west CLNG, tel: 53294044, offers 1 hr or 30 min river cruises from Puy L'Evêque, Douelle, Cahors, Laroque des Arcs and Tour de Faure. At Cahors the departure quay is on the south bank of the river. You can also hire boats on the Lot from Luzech, tel: 65917271, Douelle, tel: 65231751, Cahors, tel: 65300899, and Bouziès, tel: 65312683. Meandering down these two magnificent rivers in a *gabare* is a delight in summer.

Boétie, Etienne de la (1530-63): Born in the most beautiful house in Sarlat, he became a counsellor in the Bordeaux parliament, and met and became close friends with Montaigne (see **A-Z**). He translated works by Plutarch and Xenophon, and wrote sonnets and treatises such as *Voluntary Servitude*, which attacked the power of tyrants. He died in 1563 aged 32 and his house and statue in Sarlat are preserved as memorials to him.

Bourdeille, Pierre de (1535-1614): This soldier of fortune (who guarded Mary Queen of Scots when she was in Leith prison) had many amorous adventures, was crippled in 1589 by falling off his horse and became Abbot of Brantôme monastery. Using the pen name of Brantôme, he wrote *Ladies of Love* and *Lives of Famous Men and Great Commanders*, celebrating the lives of courtesans and warriors. See **CHATEAUX-PÉRIGUEUX 1, PÉRIGUEUX-EXCURSION 2.**

Budget: Generally speaking, prices of hotels and restaurants are less expensive in the Dordogne and Lot than in the main cities and coastal regions of France:

Hotel breakfast	25-40F
Lunch	from 60F
Plat du jour	from 25F
Museum/chateau ticket	12-30F
Bottle of *vin du patron*	35-55F
Hotel room for two	125-600F
Picnic lunch for two from supermarket	45F

Buses: There are many small local bus companies. Information is available from Tourist Offices and railway stations (SNCF).

Périgueux	Bus station, Pl. Francheville, tel: 53087600. Various routes go to Limoges (2 hr 30 min), Riberac, Sarlat (via Montignac, 2 hr), Brantôme and Bergerac (1 hr 15 min). The Tourist Office and bus station have information on schedules.
Bergerac	At SNCF, Ave du 108 RI.
Sarlat	Two main stops at SNCF station and in Pl. Pasteur. Rural routes include Trans-Périgord to Souillac, Cars Pezin to

Domme and Cars Canitrot to Gourdon. The Tourist Office publishes schedules in *Informations Générales*.

Cahors   SNCF buses in front of station.
Figeac   SNCF buses from station 500 m south of the river, in Pl. de la Gare.
Gourdon   SNCF buses from station, 500 m east of the Tourist Office.
Riberac   Outside Café du Palais, Pl. Debonnière.
Souillac   SNCF station is the main stop for Trans-Périgord and SNCF buses.

The bus *guide horaire* for the Lot department can be obtained in Cahors, tel: 65300501 or 65352512. Taking a bus is not a sophisticated journey in the Dordogne and Lot. They usually leave and arrive on time but expect to sit next to a farmer's wife with a crate of fresh eggs, or even a chicken, on her lap. SNCF organizes bus excursions from Cahors (Grottes de Cabrerets, St. Cirq-Lapopie); Figeac (*La Vallée du Célé et du Lot*); Périgueux (*Circuit des Bastides, Vallée de la Dordogne*); Bergerac (*Provencale en Périgord*); Sarlat (*La Préhistoire*, Lascaux II); and Souillac (Les Eyzies-de-Tayac, *Collonges-la-Rouge*). See **Transport**.

Cahors: Pop: 21,000. At the cross-roads of the N 20 and the D 911, Cahors is the *préfecture* town of the Lot department, and is surrounded on three sides by a great loop in the River Lot. Cahors knew fame initially as a Roman city. Then in the 13thC it became the Lombard banking centre of Europe until the English seized the town towards the end of the Hundred Years' War (see **A-Z**). The religious wars of the 16thC between Huguenots (see **A-Z**) and Catholics caused great misery. Léon Gambetta (see **A-Z**), a famous local barrister and statesman, has given his name to streets and squares all over France. The Bd Gambetta, with its many plane trees, cafés and shops, runs north-south and bisects the town. The eatern sector of the town is much more interesting, and all the major sights are there. The Tourist Office is in the Pl. Aristide Briand, tel: 65350956, a large square with chestnut trees and the departure point for local buses. Cahors is an up-and-coming tourist centre with 13 hotels, many restaurants, a camp site and excellent excursions east and west along the river valleys. The Tourist Office arranges daily tours of the *vieille ville* (1000 and 1500 in summer) and regional minibus wine tours. Ask for the newssheet *Vacances et Loisirs*. See **CAHORS**, **Boat Trips**, **Roman Sites**, **Tourist Information**.

Cameras & Photography: Films, video cassettes and flashes are widely available in all towns. Check with staff before using a camera in museums or art galleries, as there are usually restrictions.

Camping & Caravanning: In the Dordogne department there are 159 camp sites available in no less than 116 villages, and in the Lot department 107 camp sites situated in 86 villages. The choice and variety of prices and facilities is considerable. The largest sites in the Dordogne are at St. Léon-sur-Vézère (600 places), Vitrac (500) and Vieux Mareuil (500), with many more having over 300 places, whereas in the Lot camp sites are much smaller, rarely above 200 places. Like all French camp sites, they are clean, well-organized and usually have a restaurant or café, tennis courts and swimming pool. Early booking is advisable. Full details can be obtained from the Office Départemental de Tourisme de la Dordogne, 16 rue Wilson, 24000 Périgueux, tel: 53534435, and the Comité Départemental du Tourisme du Lot, BP7, 46001 Cahors, tel: 65350709. The French Government Tourist Office's address in the UK is 178 Piccadilly, London WIV OAL, tel: 071-4936594, and it also has information on camp sites.

Car Hire: To hire a car you must produce a passport and a current driving licence which has been valid for at least one year. A cash deposit is necessary unless paying by credit card, and also proof of a local (hotel) address. The minimum age is 21-25, depending on the company. Be sure to check the basis of charge, i.e. a daily rate plus so much per km, or unlimited mileage. Third-party insurance is compulsory.

Périgueux	Europcar, 14 rue Denis Papin, tel: 53081572.
	Budget Cars, 28 rue Chanzy, tel: 53098848.
Bergerac	Ford, rte Périgueux, tel: 53572141.
Sarlat	Sarlat-Autos, rte Vitrac, tel: 53591064.
Cahors	Europcar, Avis and Hertz are in Ave Jean Jaurès, opposite SNCF.
	Noyer (Renault), rte de Toulouse, tel: 65351595.
Figeac	Avis, 10 Quai Bessières, tel: 65341028.
Gourdon	Renault Garage, rte du Vigan, tel: 65411024.
	Landes, Ave Grimardet, tel: 65410647.

Chateaux & Castles: There are a thousand in the region, on hill tops, in woods – castles for military might, chateaux for social elegance. Along the River Dordogne they glare at one another much as they did in the Hundred Years' War (see **A-Z**). The best examples are northeast (Jumilhac-le-Grand, Puyguilhem, La Martonie), and east (Hautefort) of Périgueux; east (Lanquais, Baneuil) and south (Monbazillac) of Bergerac; and half a dozen near Sarlat (Beynac, Castelnaud and Biron). In the Lot department see Castelnau, Bonaguil and Montal. See **CHATEAUX**.

Chemists: There are plenty of chemists (*pharmacies*) identifiable by a green cross sign in all towns. They are usually open 0900-1930 Mon.-Sat. and have a Sunday rota which your hotel manager or Tourist Office can advise. See **Health**, **Opening Times**.

Children: They are always welcome in hotels, restaurants, cafés and museums. Activities might include visits to grottoes, boat trips on the river, the zoo at Padirac, the monkey park near Rocamadour and the butterfly park at L'Hospitalet (see **ROCAMADOUR-WHAT TO SEE**), and the reptile park at Martel. There are also pony clubs, aqua centres at Payrac, Betaille and Figeac, *Parc de Loisirs* (entertainment centres) at Varaire and Souillac, and the *roulotte à cheval* (see **A-Z**).

Churches & Abbeys: Rocamadour is an outstanding place to visit, with a series of churches and chapels clinging to a steep cliff face (see **ROCA-MADOUR-WHAT TO SEE, Rocamadour**). Périgueux, Sarlat and Cahors have cathedrals of architectural and historical interest. Cadouin's 12thC church and cloisters (see **SARLAT-EXCURSION 2**), Souillac's 12thC abbey (see **GOURDON-EXCURSION**), and the huge fortified churches of St. Amand-de-Coly, Rudelle and St. Pierre Toirac are particularly noteworthy.

Climate: The region has a mild climate in winter (9-12°C), is warm in spring and autumn (12-19°C) and usually very hot in midsummer (19-27°C). Fortunately the many rivers, lakes and wooded landscapes keep the climate equable and the air pure. The best time to go is in the spring or autumn simply because the hotels and camp sites get very full in midsummer with French, English and Dutch tourists.

Complaints: It is very rare in the Dordogne and Lot to be over-charged in hotels or restaurants, but nevertheless check every bill as you would at home. Ensure that if you have chosen a fixed-price menu (there may be several), the waiter does know which one you have selected: 'Le menu à 110F svp'. Taxis may take you by a longer route than is strictly necessary! If you have a serious complaint take it immediately to the manager of the establishment. If you get no satisfaction go to the Tourist Office and only as a final resort go to the police. See **Police**, **Tourist Information**.

Consulates:

UK	15 cours de Verdun, Bordeaux 33081, tel: 56522835.
USA	22 cours du Maréchal Foch, Bordeaux 33080, tel: 56526595.

Conversion Charts:

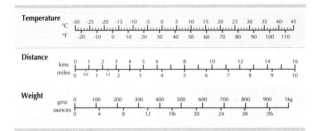

Craft Courses: Organized by local craftsmen (*artisans*), holiday courses abound in the region. Activities include archaeology, painting, sculpture, weaving, ironwork, basketwork, pottery, cooking and many others. The Tourist Office will advise you on what is available, although advance booking from the UK is recommended.

Credit Cards: See **Money**.

Crime & Theft: Never leave your car unlocked and be sure to remove or hide any valuables. If you do have anything stolen, report the theft immediately to the nearest police station (*commissariat de police*) and obtain an *attestation de vol* document so that you can claim insurance. You must inform your consulate at once if your passport is stolen. See **Consulates, Emergency Numbers, Insurance, Police**.

Croquants: In 1594, oppressed by poverty, heavy taxes, famine and an overbearing nobility, the peasants (*Croquants*) revolted and over the next half-century minor pitched battles took place at St. Crépin-d'Auberoche, St. Condat-sur-Vézère, Ste-Foy-La-Grande and La Sauvetat. Eventually their weaver leader Buffarot, from Capdrot, was captured and brutally killed in the main square of the *bastide* town of Monpazier in 1637. Another uprising in 1642 also failed. See PÉRIGUEUX-EXCURSION 1.

Currency: The French unit of currency is the franc, which divides into 100 centimes. Bank notes are issued for 500F, 200F, 100F, 50F and 20F. Coins are 10F (two types, the older version is bronze-coloured, the newer ones are smaller with a brass rim and silver centre), 5F, 2F, 1F, 50c (all silver), 20c, 10c and 5c (all brass). See **Money**.

Customs Allowances:

Duty Paid Into:	Cigarettes	or	Cigars	or	Tobacco	Spirits	or	Wine
EC	300		75		400g	1.5 l		5 l
UK	300		75		400g	1.5 l		5 l

Dentists: See **Health**.

Disabled Travellers: For information about accommodation, transport, facilities and aids for the disabled, see the booklets *Touristes Quand Même* and *Guide des transports à l'usage des personnes à mobilité réduite* supplied by the Tourist Office. All TGV high-speed trains can accommodate wheelchairs, and guide dogs are transported free. Other trains have a special compartment and an escalator for boarding. See **Health**, **Insurance**, **Tourist Information**.

Doctors: See **Emergency Numbers**, **Health**.

Drinks: In France there are no licensing laws, so you can buy alcohol in bars and cafés at any time. House wines are sold by the litre (*une carafe*), half litre (*un demi-litre*) or quarter litre (*un quart*); a jug (*un pichet*) can hold either a quarter or half litre. Beer is usually lager. At meals plain water (*une carafe d'eau*) comes free. Coffee: ask for *un café* for a small strong black espresso, *un café au lait* for coffee with milk, and *un grand crème* for a large white coffee. Tea is available at *salons de thé*, and hot chocolate – *un chocolat* – is popular. Drinks are less expensive served standing in a bar or café (*au comptoir*) than seated. A pavement table may cost you a great deal more. See **Wines**.

Driving: Apart from rush-hour traffic in the big towns, driving in the Dordogne and Lot is usually a pleasure, particularly out of season. You will need a valid national or international driving licence plus comprehensive insurance documents (preferably a Green Card), nationality sticker, yellow filters for headlamps and a red warning triangle. The French drive on the right-hand side of the road, and at T-junctions, intersections and roundabouts the traffic from the right has priority. The wearing of seatbelts is compulsory for passengers in the front and recommended for those in the back. Try to make long journeys by car on a Sunday when trucks are forbidden by law. Speed limits: built-up areas 60 kph; main roads 90-110 kph; motorways (*autoroutes*) 130 kph. Speeding offences carry a large on-the-spot fine from motorway police. French drivers are very competitive and a foreign numberplate is a challenge; to be resisted. Petrol (*l'essence*) is available by the litre and prices are clearly marked in petrol stations, which are usually self-service. Parking meters operate 0900-1900 and police or traffic wardens can impose fines or tow away vehicles parked illegally. If impounded telephone the town hall (*mairie*) to reclaim your vehicle. See **Accidents & Breakdowns**, **Car Hire**.

Drugs: In France it is illegal to use or possess any form of narcotic, and anyone caught trying to smuggle drugs into the country faces almost certain imprisonment.

Eating Out: By law all restaurants must display their prices outside and have at least one fixed-price menu (*menu fixe, rapide menu, menu touristique*), as well as the 'à la carte'. These fixed-price menus for two or three courses can cost as little as 50F, whereas the 'à la carte' is always more expensive. The *plat du jour* is usually good, so ask the waiter what it is. Restaurants traditionally serve lunch from midday and rarely after 1400, and the evening meal from 1930-2100, but brasseries, bistros and *le drugstore* will serve a *plat du jour* at almost any time. Cafés serve a variety of drinks all day, as well as snacks, sandwiches and *croque-monsieur* (a toasted ham and cheese sandwich). Every Tourist Office will have a list of local restaurants, with addresses, telephone numbers, style of cuisine and some indication of

price. In the topics section of this guide an inexpensive meal would cost 50-100F, a moderate meal 100-200F and an expensive meal over 200F. See **RESTAURANTS-BERGERAC, CAHORS, PÉRIGUEUX, SARLAT, Drinks, Food, Tipping**.

Eleanor of Aquitaine (1122-1204): Married in 1137 when she was 15, to the French King Louis VII, this remarkable woman had inherited the huge prosperous region of Aquitaine from her father. Eventually, after 15 years, the marriage was annulled, and the young and beautiful woman – a great favourite of the court troubadours (see **A-Z**) – married Henry Plantagenet, Duke of Normandy and future King of England. They were crowned in Westminster Abbey in 1154 and for the next three centuries Britain ruled Aquitaine, which included the regions of Périgord and Quercy.

Electricity: The voltage in France is 220V and a two-pin adaptor is required, available from most electrical shops.

Emergency Numbers:

Police		17
Fire brigade (*sapeurs pompiers*)		18
Périgueux SAMU (24-hr ambulance)		53088111
Hospitals:		
Périgueux	80 Ave Georges Pompidou	53077000
Bergerac	Bd du Prof-Calmette	53577777
Sarlat	rue Jean Leclaire	53590072
Cahors	rue Président Wilson	65354797
Figeac	33 rue Maquisards	65342270
Gourdon	Ave Pasteur	65410104

For ambulances use the number given in the telephone box or, if no number is given, call the police (*brigade de gendarmerie*). There are emergency telephones approximately every 20 km on main roads and these are connected direct to the local police stations which operate 24 hours a day. In larger towns emergency help is available from the *police secours* (Emergency Assistance Department).

Events: Every town and village has its *fête votive* (saint's day) during the summer, an occasion for a fair (with circus roundabouts), a *bal* (dancing in the main square to loud unsophisticated music), possibly a *fête champêtre* (town or village lunch or supper in the streets or park: open to anyone, at a low price) and probably ending with *feu de St. Jean* (fireworks). Few notable events take place in the region outside the summer season, which starts in June and ends in September. Each year a special festival takes place at a different venue in the regions of Périgord Blanc (NE), Périgord Vert (NW), Périgord Pourpre (SW) and Périgord Noir (E), in relation to Périgueux, usually in the period 20 July-30 August. A similar event occurs in the Lot, in Quercy Blanc (E) and Quercy Noir (W). Each year a town or large village is picked to celebrate the Felibrée, an important folklore event, with everyone in traditional dress, town decorations, and dancing and singing in the streets. Ask the Tourist Office for a *calendrier* of local events.

Spring: Mardi Gras (Shrove Tuesday) is celebrated in Périgueux, and to a lesser extent in the smaller towns.

June: Bergerac has jazz concerts throughout the summer either in the Cloître des Recollets or the Pl. St. Jacques; the Festival of Pictorial Art is held in the Centre Artistique des Cordeliers; the Music Festival has weekly concerts in the Centre Culturelle from late June to September. A series of folklore events also takes place throughout the summer season. Périgueux also starts its season of cultural events in June, but Sarlat has the edge with its Musique en Sarlaidais.

July: Cahors hosts its Blues Festival in the first week, and Souillac has a Jazz Festival in July and August. Sarlat starts its Theatre Festival in mid-July for a month, held either in the Centre Culturelle or Theâtre Municipal (next door to the Cathedral). Figeac and St. Céré also have summer festivals of music, dance, concerts and folklore from mid-July. Rocamadour has *Son et Lumière*, as does Cadouin Abbey. Bergerac has a Folklore Festival, and Bonaguil has not only a Music Festival but *Son et Lumière* too; *14:* Périgueux has processions and fireworks along the River L'Isle. Every town celebrates the 14th in various ways; *21-mid August:* Montignac has a Festival Amicale Laique of folklore; *25:* Gourdon has an International Music Festival held in the churches of St. Pierre and Notre Dame des Cordeliers.

August: Most of July's events carry on into August, but in addition, in the Lot there is the Quercy Blanc and Noir Festival, and Périgueux has MIMOS, a mime festival, in the first two weeks, followed by two weeks of pantomime. Nontron has Folklore d'Europe in the first week. Other events include a Harvest Festival in Gourdon and a Drama and Theatre Festival in Sarlat.

September: Rocamadour has a major pilgrimage in the week of the 8th, attended by thousands.

See **Folklore**, **Music**, **Sports**.

Fénelon (1651-1715): Born in the 14thC chateau of the same name, near Ste-Mondane, he became Archbishop of Cambrai and a royal tutor, but was disgraced by the publication of *Télémaque* which was thought to be an indiscreet political satire. He was senior Prior of Carennac for the last 15 years of his banishment. See **CHATEAUX-SARLAT & GOURDON 1**.

Figeac: Pop: 11,000. The second town in the Lot department, on the north bank of the River Célé, Figeac grew in importance during the Middle Ages as it was on the pilgrim route to Santiago de Compostela in northwest Spain. More recently it suffered in World War II when the activities of the Resistance movement provoked the Germans into deporting 600 citizens. The town was awarded the *Croix de Guerre* for this disaster.

It has an old quarter of 13th-15thC gold sandstone houses, a 13thC mint which also houses the Tourist Office, two small museums and an 11thC abbey. The River Célé runs east-west through the town and there are three bridges spanning it. Five major roads converge on Figeac: the N 140 from Brive and Tulle in the north, the N 122 from Aurillac in the east, the N 140 from Rodez to the southeast, the D 922 from Villefranche-de-Rouergue to the south and the D 13 from the west. A good centre for excursions, Figeac has ten hotels and two camp sites. You can also eat well in the town's excellent restaurants on river trout, truffles, *cèpes*, foie gras and walnuts. Enclos de Carmes is expensive, Champollion is moderately priced and La Croix Blanche inexpensive. See **FIGEAC**, **Tourist Information**.

Fishing: This is a popular pastime along the many rivers, but you will need a temporary licence or permit – ask for information at the Tourist Office. Trout, roach, perch, bream, pike, tench and carp are the local fish. Some of the best fishing lakes are around Nontron (Étang de St. Estèphe) and south of Riberac in the Double and Landais regions. The two departmental fishing offices are at 182 quai Cavaignac, Cahors, tel: 65355022 and at 7 rue du Lys, Périgueux, tel: 53534421.

Folklore: Preservation of local customs, dress, language, dance and song is widely encouraged. There are two societies near Périgueux: Lou Chabridous, 43 rue des Pinsons, N-D-de-Sanilhac, tel: 53090820, and Los Croquants d'Escornabiou, Sarazy Coulounieux, tel: 53084271. Bergerac has a *spectacle folklorique* in Pl. St. Jacques during the summer. Sarlat's *groupe folklorique* is called Les Pastoureaux Sarladais. Nontron hosts a Folklore d'Europe festival in early August. Each year in July a different town celebrates the Felibrée and is decorated with brightly-coloured paper flowers forming triumphal arches in the streets. Hundreds of visitors parade dressed in traditional costume, a 'queen' is elected, and there are speeches followed by Mass and a banquet (*fête champêtre*) in the open air. Mussidan maintains a permanent Felibrée museum, assembled by Dr André Voulgre in his 19thC town house. It includes artisan workshops, exhibition hall, old agricultural machinery and several furnished rooms typical of a bygone era. See **Events**, **Mussidan**.

Food: On a visit to any village on market day you will see the colourful local produce. This land of milk and honey has nearly 100,000 farms with sheep, pigs, geese and ducks producing superlative delicacies. Foie gras (goose liver) appears on most menus, as a pâté, or served hot or cold in slices. *Confit de canard, d'oie, de porc* or *de dinde* are pieces of duck, goose, pork or turkey salted, then cooked and preserved in their own fat in earthenware jars.

Cassoulet à la Périgourdine consists of sausages, bits of pork and white haricot beans. *Sobronade* is a thick stew-soup including onions, carrots, turnips, leeks and celery, and spiced with herbs and garlic. *Poulet rouilleuse* is chicken cooked in a rich white wine and garlic sauce, thickened with chicken blood. *Dodines de volaille* are boned, marinated chicken, stuffed and braised. *Tourtière* is chicken and salsify pie, and *daube* is a rich beef stew. Rabbit (*lapin*), hare (*lièvre*), duck (*canard*) and guinea fowl (*pintarde*) appear frequently on menus, with local mushrooms, *cèpes* and truffles. *Cabecou* is a Quercy goat cheese from Gramat with which to drink your Cahors wine. *Pastis* is a gateau with sliced apples. Fresh river fish (trout, salmon, perch) are popular too, preceded by *garbure*, a peasants' vegetable soup. You will see walnut trees everywhere, and rich walnut cakes made by the *grandes pâtisseries* in Cahors make a good present for taking home. See **Eating Out**, **Markets**.

Gambetta, Léon (1838-82): Born in Cahors, he studied law in Paris, became a member of the Legislative Assembly, helped topple Napolean III, fought the Prussians and escaped from Paris in a balloon. Eventually he became prime minister and a national hero, with hundreds of streets named after him. See **Cahors**.

Gourdon: Pop: 5000. Gourdon, capital of the region known as *La Bouriane*, stands at the crossroads of the D 704 (northwest to Sarlat, south to Cahors) and the D 673 (west to Salviac and Cazals, east to Payrac, Rocamadour and Gramat). There is an old town, Hôtel de Ville, the 14thC church of St. Pierre and an esplanade with good views of the valleys of the Dordogne and Céou. The town is also on the main railway between Toulouse, Cahors and Paris and is an excellent centre for excursions to the major sights of Rocamadour, Padirac, the grottoes and chateaux. There are ten hotels, two camp sites and a wide choice of restaurants; La Croque-Note, La Bouriane and Terminus are all moderately priced. *Confit d'oie*, river trout, Causse leg of mutton, jugged hare and *pastis* are local specialities. See **GOURDON**, **Tourist Information**.

Health: Free medical treatment is available to all citizens of EC countries. Residents of the UK should obtain a form E 111 from the DSS before departure. You will have to pay for any treatment in the first place, then claim it back afterwards. Even an ordinary visit to the doctor costs about 100F, so it certainly pays to take out medical insurance beforehand. Lists of doctors and dentists, including those available on Sundays and holidays, can be obtained from police stations, chemists and probably from your hotel. See **Disabled Travellers**, **Emergency Numbers**, **Insurance**.

Holiday Villages: The French have an up-market version of the British holiday camp, set in the countryside, where a cluster of chalets, usually near a lake, offer every variety of mildly organized holiday activity; tennis, swimming, riding, cycling, children's activities, etc. In the Dordogne department the villages are at Lapeyre (north of Nontron), Clairvivre, Salagnac (northeast of Hautefort), Milhac de Nontron, Jumilhac-le-Grand, St. Crépin-Carlucet, St. Estèphe, Loubejac and Tremolat. The Lot has eight such villages; Cajarc, tel: 65406739, Castelfranc, tel: 65362038, Gluges Martel, tel: 65373370, Gourdon, tel: 65410515, Prayssac, tel: 65224198. St. Chamarand, tel: 65310016, and two at Vers, tel: 65314029 and 65314174.

Hospitals: See **Emergency Numbers**.

Hôtels: The elegant town mansions called *hôtels*, dating from the 17th-18thC, and still surviving in Sarlat, Périgueux and Figeac as well as other towns, were built for the nobility and judiciary. Architects were often influenced by the graceful Italian style. See **PÉRIGUEUX-WALK 2, WHAT TO SEE, SARLAT-WALK, WHAT TO SEE.**

House Purchase: Over 5000 British families own properties in the region, either as *maisons secondaires* or as retirement homes. Attracted by the agreeable climate, good food and wine at reasonable cost they settle – more peaceably than their forebears during the Hundred Years' War (see **A-Z**) – around towns such as Riberac, Eymet and Cahors. French estate agents, *agents immobiliers*, still have many properties on their books. Certain UK agents also handle purchases without extra cost. But do visit an area out of season and make a wide-ranging search before committing yourself. See **Mussidan**.

Huguenots: Protesters against the excesses of the Catholic Church in the early 16thC in Périgord and Quercy were called Huguenots. The first Huguenot martyr was burnt at the stake at Ste-Foy-La-Grande in 1542. Bergerac was a major Huguenot centre and in 1572, during the Massacre of St. Bartholomew, thousands of Huguenots were brutally killed here. Geoffroi de Vivans was the famous Huguenot leader in Périgord. Indeed, Périgueux, Domme and other towns were captured by him. He is buried at Doissat, near Belvès. Château Montfort was a Huguenot refuge and many of the prehistory sites south of Montignac were used to hide fleeing Huguenots. Following Louis XIV's 1685 Revocation of the Edict of Nantes thousands emigrated to Britain, the Netherlands and Switzerland, denuding the country of skills.

Hundred Years' War (1345-1453): The many castles along the frontier of the River Dordogne, the *bastide* towns (see **A-Z**) and the final battle site at Castillon (see **BERGERAC-EXCURSION 2**) are visible legacies of our longest war.

Insurance: You should take out comprehensive travel insurance covering you and your family, if travelling with you, against theft and loss of property, car and money, as well as medical expenses, for the duration of your stay. Your travel agent, the AA or RAC will recommend a suitable policy. See **Crime & Theft**, **Driving**, **Health**.

Knights Templars: With the end of the Crusades in 1291 many rich and successful knights returned from the Holy Land and settled in France. In Périgord and Quercy they founded commanderies and preceptories at Sergeac, Jumilhac-le-Grand (see CHATEAUX-PÉRIGUEUX 2), Allemans, Condat-sur-Vézère and a score of other villages. Their influence was beneficial but the popes were so jealous of these soldier-knights and their religious activities that the French King was persuaded to abolish the Order in 1312 and confiscate all of its possessions. In Domme you can still see the graffiti on the prison walls written in despair by the Templar prisoners.

Lascaux: In September 1940, schoolboys searching for a lost dog a few kilometres southeast of Montignac, discovered the world's most interesting prehistoric cave. Dating from the Magdalenian period of 17,000 years ago this cave, 150 m long, contains 1500 painted or engraved wall scenes of bulls, cows, bison, reindeer, wild horses and a human hunter. Opened to the public in 1948, Lascaux attracted millions of visitors from all over the world. Due to deterioration through humidity and carbon dioxide it was closed in 1963. Lascaux II is an astonishing modern man-made replica constructed 200 m from the original cave. See PREHISTORY-MUSEUMS, SITES, SARLAT-EXCURSION 1, **Prehistory**.

Laundries: Hotels will usually do your laundry. Most towns in the Dordogne and Lot now have self-service, coin-operated launderettes (*laundromats, laverie automatique*), usually open 0800-1900.

Les Eyzies-de-Tayac: The major centre for prehistory in the Vézère river valley. The Cro-Magnon shelter, Font de Gaume and the Musée National de Préhistoire make this small town an interesting visit for all the family. The 11thC chateau clings to the cliffs overlooking the town, and near the SNCF is a huge 12thC fortified church. There are nine hotels, many restaurants and two camp sites. The Tourist Office is in the Pl. de la Mairie, tel: 53069705. See **PREHISTORY-MUSEUMS**, **SITES**, **Prehistory**.

Lost Property: If you lose anything you should contact the Bureau des Objets Trouvés.

Markets: Every French town has its market, usually to be found in the main square in front of the Cathedral on Wednesday and Saturday, starting at about 0800 and finishing at lunchtime. Fruit, vegetables, flowers and poultry are displayed on open stalls along with delicacies such as honey-comb, truffles, walnuts and walnut oil, *cèpes*, freshwater fish, dozens of different cheeses and, of course, *confits d'oie* and pâté from duck and goose. Look out for *pastis*, tarts made of crystallized fruit and walnut cake. See **Food, Tourist Information**.

Money: Every town has a wide choice of banks which open 0900-1630 Mon.-Fri. There are exchange facilities at airports and main-line railway stations as well as in most Tourist Offices (useful at weekends). Most main post offices have currency exchange facilities, often with a low rate of commission. Cities have a number of bureaux de change in the centre and near the SNCF. Exchange rates and commission charges vary, so it pays to look around. Credit cards are widely accepted, with Visa (*Carte Bleu*) being the most common. Traveller's cheques are probably the safest way to carry holiday money, and can be used in many locations but not in the smaller hotels and restaurants. They are easy to change at any bank or bureau de change. See **Currency**.

Montaigne, Michel de (1533-92): Educated in Bordeaux by George Buchanan, the Scottish humanist, Montaigne became a counsellor in the Cour des Aides at Périgueux, practised law and retired early, on his father's death, to the family chateau and estate of St. Michel-de-Montaigne a few kilometres north of Montcaret. There he wrote essays and tracts in the midst of the savage religious wars, advocating tolerance and reason. Sayings for which he is remembered are, 'Why this rather than that?', 'Neither wish nor fear your last day' and *'Que sais-je?'* – What do I know?

Montfort, Simon de (1208-65): This brilliant soldier, adventurer and fanatic was born into a rich family and bestowed with a dozen titles, including Lord of Montfort, Evreux, Béziers and Carcassonne. He became notorious for burning and destroying many towns, villages and chateaux in Périgord and Quercy, and was the scourge of the wretched Albigensian heretics.

Murat, General Joachim (1767-1815): Son of an innkeeper at Labastide-Fortuniere (northeast of Cahors), he became one of Napoleon's trusted marshals and King of Naples. Renowned for his bravery – a rare general who led from the front – he suffered an inglorious death as a traitor. The name of the village was changed to Labastide-Murat in his honour, and a small museum is in the house where he was born.

Museums: There are 50 museums in the region: 32 in the Dordogne, 18 in the Lot. Some unusual museums in the Dordogne are: Auriac-du-Périgord (bees), Bergerac (tobacco), Les Eyzies-de-Tayac (pot-holing and medicinal plants), Monbazillac (Protestantism), Nontron (dolls and puppets), Périgueux (military history), Sarlat (fishermen's traditions), Sorges (truffles) and Villefranche-du-Périgord (mushrooms and chestnuts). In the Lot department there are interesting museums at Rocamadour (sacred art), St. Céré (tapestries), Labastide-Murat (General Murat) and Cabrerets (prehistory). Times and charges for admission are liable to alteration. Most are closed on Tuesday, some on Monday. Usual hours are 1000-1200 and 1400-1700. Many smaller museums are closed out of season. Sunday openings are often free of charge. Consult the Tourist Office for current opening hours and scale of admission prices.

Music: The major towns of Périgueux, Bergerac, Sarlat and Cahors have a long summer season of musical events between July and September. Other towns with music venues include Bonaguil, Le Bugue, Brantôme, Gourdon and St. Céré, and the villages of St. Amand-de-Coly, St. Léon-sur-Vézère, St. Astier, Jumilhac-le-Grand, Couze, Chancelade, St. Jean-de-Côle and Villefranche-du-Périgord. Music lovers should ask the Tourist Office for the season's *Manifestations Culturelles*. See **Events, Tourist Information**.

Mussidan: Pop: 3200. 35 km southwest of Périgueux on the N 89. On the banks of the River L'Isle, it is popular with British property buyers. The André Voulgre Museum of Popular Arts and Folklore is well worth a visit (1000-1200, 1400-1800 Wed.-Mon., mid June-mid Sep., rest of year weekends only: 14F). See **Folklore, House Purchase**.

Newspapers: English newspapers are available, one day after publication, in *librairies* (book and newspaper shops) and some kiosks.

Nightlife: The Dordogne and Lot have few sophisticated nightclubs, although there are cinemas, some theatres and discos.

Périgueux

Theatre:	Palais des Fêtes, Ave d'Aquitaine, tel: 53531871.
	Café St. Louis, 26 bis rue Eguillerie, off Bd Montaigne, 2000-0200 Mon.-Sat. Sometimes features live jazz.
Discos:	L'An des Roys, 52 rue Aubarede, tel: 53530158. 2230-0230 Wed.-Sat.
	L'Ubu, 3 rue des Jacobins, tel: 53092902. 2200-0300 Tue.-Sun. *Club privé*, may need introduction.
	La Régence, 16 rue Chancelier-de-l'Hôpital, tel: 53531055.
Cinemas:	Marignan, 17 cours Montaigne.
	Le Paris, Pl. Francheville.
	Le Rex, 30 rue Gambetta.
	Le Montaigne, cours Montaigne.
Bergerac	Disco Le Windsor, rte de Bordeaux, tel: 53576660. Thu.-Sun.: 15F, Sat. 60F. Two discos: one for the young, the other for the not-so-young.
	Le Nouvel Espace, Château Mounet-Sully, rte de Mussidan, tel: 53632480. Tue.-Sun.: 45F, Sat. 55F.
	Le Prince, rte d'Agen, tel: 53574956. Late-night restaurant 2000-0400 Wed.-Mon., disco 2230-0400: 45F, Sat. 55F.
Sarlat	Open-air theatre in Pl. de la Liberté.
Cahors	Disco Babys Club, Pl. des Consuls, tel: 65220695.
	Le Manakin, rte de Toulouse, tel: 65300763.
	Le Look, rte de Paris, tel: 65225719.
Figeac	L'Axye Pub, Ave Pompidou, tel: 65341991.
	Chateau Ceint d'Eau, tel: 65342342.

In most cases you should check opening times with the Tourist Office beforehand. See **Tourist Information**.

Nontron: Pop: 4000. A busy commercial town on the D 675 49 km north of Périgueux, overlooking the valley of the River Bandiat and surrounded by lakes. The 18thC chateau near the impressive ramparts houses an unusual folklore and doll museum (open all year, closed Tue. out of season: 12F). Good hotels, and camping and fishing facilities.

Opening Times:
Banks – 0900-1200, 1400-1630 Mon.-Fri. (busy central branches stay open at lunchtime).
Chemists – 0830-1200, 1400-1800 Mon.-Sat. (a Sun. roster usually operates).
Churches – In towns 0800-1800, but closed 1200-1400 in villages.
Currency Exchange (bureau de change) – Times vary from 0830/0900/0930-1800/2200 Mon.-Sat.
Offices – 0830-1200, 1400-1800 Mon.-Sat.
Post Offices – 0800-1900 Mon.-Fri., 0800-1200 Sat.
Restaurants – Usually 1200-1430, 1900-2200. Many close on Mon., and some close for August and a winter month.
Shops – Vary enormously between 0800-1900, with smaller shops closing for lunch between 1200-1400. Others may close on Mon.

Parking: See **Driving**.

Passports & Customs: A passport from Britain, Ireland or the EC allows a 90-day stay with no visa required. Also acceptable are British visitors' passports and excursion passes (available from post offices). If you wish to stay for more than 90 days contact the local French police station (*commissariat de police*). Citizens from other countries, including the USA, Canada, Australia and New Zealand, require a visa which is easily obtained from French embassies and consulates in those countries. See **Customs Allowances**.

Périgueux: Pop: 36,000. The *préfecture* town of the Dordogne department, with the interesting sectors situated west of the River L'Isle. The view from the river bridge of the many Byzantine cupolas of the Cathédrale de St. Front is stunning. The medieval town, now mainly pedestrianized, with old *hôtels* (see **A-Z**) and smart shops and cafés, is within walking distance of the Cathedral. The remains of the Roman town are 1 km west, near the Église de St. Etienne-de-la-Cité. Périgueux is noted for its fine cuisine and is also a cultural centre, with two museums, an Art Festival and a good programme of music, folklore exhibitions and pantomime. Interesting tours can be made north to Nontron

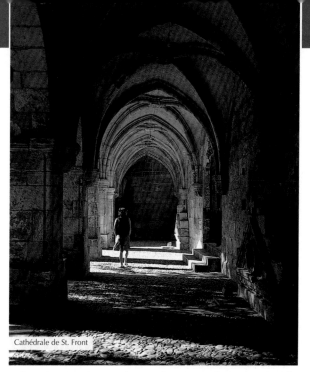
Cathédrale de St. Front

and exquisite Brantôme, northeast and east to see chateaux, and south-east to the prehistoric grottoes around Montignac. There are 24 hotels, many good restaurants and five camp sites nearby. See **PÉRIGUEUX**, **Events**, **Roman Sites**, **Tourist Information**.

Petrol: See **Driving**.

Police: They can be recognized by their dark blue uniforms and flat caps. Always address them as *Monsieur l'Agent* – they are usually help-ful to tourists. Any theft should be reported to the nearest police station (*commissariat de police*).

Périgueux   rue du 4 Septembre, tel: 53081767.
Bergerac   Bd Chanzy, tel: 53576102.
Sarlat   Pl. Grand Rigandie, tel: 53590517.
Cahors   rue St. Gèry, tel: 65352700.
Figeac   Cité Admin., Carmes, tel: 65341717.
Gourdon   15 allées République, tel: 65410781.
Souillac   rte de Sarlat, tel: 65327817.
See **Crime & Theft**, **Emergency Numbers**.

Post Offices: Look for their yellow signs marked PTT or POSTES
(post boxes are the same colour). They provide full postal services, and
telephones for both local and long-distance calls. These can be
metered and paid for afterwards. Often a currency exchange service is
available. Postage stamps can also be purchased from *tabacs*.
Main post offices:
Périgueux   rue du 4 Septembre (near Tourist Office), tel: 53533703.
Bergerac   rue de la Résistance, tel: 53571207.
Sarlat   Pl. du 14 Juillet, tel: 53591281.
Cahors   257 rue Wilson, tel: 65354089.
Figeac   Ave F. Pezet, tel: 65346314.
Souillac   11 Bd Louis-Jean Malvy, tel: 65378281.
See **Opening Times**, **Telephones & Telegrams**.

Prehistory: Over 200 sites revealing much about the evolution of
man have been found in Périgord-Dordogne. The Neolithic era (7500
years ago) of Homo sapiens included several 'human' types named
after places in the region. 'Cro-Magnon' man came from a cave discovered in 1868 between Tayac and Les Eyzies-de-Tayac. The tall strongly-
formed bone structure was similar to the African Berber tribes.
'Chancelade' man was discovered when skeletons were excavated in
1888 at Chancelade, a site 5 km northwest of Périgueux. The
Mongoloid cranium was considered to be pure Eskimo! Other names
include 'Mousterian' (Le Moustier), 'Magdalenian' (La Madeleine) and
'Périgordian' man. The valley of the Vézère from Montignac southwest
to Le Bugue contains many important prehistory sites. See
PREHISTORY, **Lascaux**, **Les Eyzies-de-Tayac**.

Grotte des Merveilles, near Rocamadour

Chapelle Notre Dame de Rocamadour

Public Holidays: 1 Jan. (New Year's Day); Easter Monday; 1 May (Labour Day); 8 May; Ascension Day (40 days after Easter); Whit Monday; 14 July; 15 Aug. (Assumption); 11 Nov.; 25 Dec. (Christmas Day). Banks close at noon on the working day before a public holiday, while most food shops close on the Mon., but remain open on Sun. am.

Rabies: Still exists in this region as in other parts of the Continent. As a precaution have all animal bites treated immediately by a doctor.

Railways: The main lines pass through Périgueux, Sarlat, Gourdon and Cahors, and connections are easy to Bordeaux, Toulouse and Paris. SNCF stations:

Périgueux rue Denis Papin (west side of town), tel: 53095058.
6-7 trains to Paris (5 hr); 11-12 to Bordeaux (1 hr 15 min); 6-8 to Toulouse (4 hr).
Bergerac Ave du 108 RI, tel: 53572671.
Sarlat rte de Souillac, 24200, tel: 53590021.
4 trains to Périgueux (1 hr 30 min); 3 to Bordeaux (2 hr 45 min).
Cahors Ave Jean Jaurès, tel: 65225050.
7 trains to Paris (5-6 hr); 12 to Toulouse (1 hr 15 min).
Figeac Ave de la Gare, tel: 65341037.
Gourdon Ave de la Gare, tel: 65410219.
See **Transport**.

Religious Services: France is predominantly a Catholic country and details and times of services can be obtained from the town Tourist Office. See **Tourist Information**.

Richard Coeur de Lion (1157-99): An inadequate King of England, a foolhardy warrior adored by the court troubadours (see **A-Z**) of Périgord; what time he spent in France was occupied with sacking castles, including Talleyrand at Excideuil (see **CHATEAUX-PÉRIGUEUX 2**), Puy-St.-Front, Beynac (see **CHATEAUX-SARLAT & GOURDON 1**) and Luzech. Before he was killed at the siege of Chalus he made a pilgrimage to the Holy Shroud of Cadouin (see **SARLAT-EXCURSION 2**).

Rocamadour: Pop: 900. For seven centuries this has been one of the major pilgrimage sites in France – indeed in Europe. This, the 'Deuxième site de France' consists of a spectacular cliff face 200 m high with its village, ramparts, a fort, numerous chapels and basilicas (each with an extraordinary history), three museums at its foot, and on the summit at L'Hospitalet, overlooking the Alzou valley, a butterfly park, an eagles' nest and a monkey park. The great annual pilgrimage to the second site in France (after Lourdes) attracts hundreds of thousands of the faithful, particularly in the week of 8 September. Rocamadour is best reached from Gourdon 36 km to the west or St. Céré 29 km to the northeast. Try to visit out of season. See **ROCAMADOUR-WHAT TO SEE.**

Roman Sites: The remains of a Roman town to the west of Périgueux are the region's most significant legacies of the Pax Romana. Known as Vesunna it was the capital of the Petrocorii tribe at the time of the Roman occupation. Similarly Cahors, capital of the Caduici tribe, was known as Divona Cadurcorum. See **PÉRIGUEUX-WALK 2**, **WHAT TO SEE**, **Cahors**.

Roulotte à Cheval: Renting a horse-drawn caravan with well-trained nag is an idyllic way to see the countryside. A family of two adults plus one or two children can rent a *roulotte à cheval* from Faux (southeast of Bergerac) and Quinsac (north of Périgueux). The season is April-Oct. and rental can be for a day, a weekend, a week or more. High season weekly rental is about 4000F. Two-day weekends start at 1000F. A five-page 'horse maintenance' manual is provided, plus three pages of advice for you, the driver. The horse becomes your friend, part of the family and your responsibility. In the Lot caravans can be rented from Attelages de la Vallée du Lot, Domaine de la Taillade, Duravel 46700 Puy L'Evêque, tel: 65365353, and Domaine de Pech-Petit, 46230 Cremps, tel: 65316061.

Roy, Eugène le (1836-1907): Dordogne's greatest 19thC novelist. Born near Hautefort chateau, he became a tax-collector at Montignac. His masterpiece, published in 1899 as *La Forêt Barade*, but which later became *Jacquou le Croquant*, recounts the miseries of peasant life of the 14thC Jacquerie and 15th-16thC *Croquants* (see **A-Z**). He wrote many other novels based on pastoral egalitarianism and was dubbed 'The Balzac of the Dordogne'. See **PÉRIGUEUX-EXCURSION 1**.

Sarlat: Pop: 11,000. The third, and most attractive, town of the Dordogne department, 10 km north of the river. The old town on the east side of the Ave Gambetta, which unfortunately bisects the main town, has been beautifully restored since 1964. Sights include the 300-year-old Cathedral, several 16thC town *hôtels* (see **A-Z**), a curious 'Lantern of the Dead', two museums and, from mid-July to mid-August, a celebrated folklore festival, La Vie en Périgord. The Saturday market displays many colourful foodstuffs – foie gras, truffles, walnuts and live

poultry – indicating culinary delights *à table*. Henry Miller called this town 'Paradis des Français'. Fourteen hotels and seven camp sites are proof of the town's tourist-pulling power, and excursions are available west to see the castles overlooking the river, northwest to see prehistoric sites on the Vézère, southwest to *bastide* country (see **A-Z**) and south to Domme and Château Biron. See **SARLAT**, **Events**, **Tourist Information**.

Shopping: All the towns featured have good shopping facilities. The larger superstores (*les grands surfaces*) tend to be sited outside town centres. They have a choice of food and wine that will suit everyone's taste and pocket. Preserved duck or goose in cans or jars and expensive truffles or foie gras make good presents. However, most of the wines of Bergerac, Monbazillac and Cahors can be purchased in the UK (see **Wines**). In Périgueux and Nontron one can buy porcelain and enamelware which derives from Limoges. Reproductions of Lascaux (see **A-Z**) and other famous prehistoric cave paintings also make unusual gifts. Many villages in the countryside sell artisan products: pottery, ceramics, paintings, sculptures, carpets, ironwork, etc. Périgueux has permanent exhibition galleries in rue Aubergerie and at 4 rue St. Front, and Sarlat at Berkenza, rue Escande. Some villages have popular *expositions artisanales* in midsummer, i.e. Brantôme, Les Eyzies-de-Tayac, Varaignes. Ask at the Tourist Office for venues, and for visits to *ateliers*, the working studios.

Smoking: Smoking is not permitted in churches, museums, art galleries and theatres, and discouraged in restaurants. Trains have separate non-smoking compartments.

Sports: Spectator sports include football, sometimes rugby, tennis tournaments, equestrian events, fishing, *pétanque* or *boules*, handball, cycle races, even baseball.

Tennis – Every town and many large villages have good quality hard courts run by the Municipal Council.

Cycling – See **Bicycle & Motorcycle Hire**.

Golf – 9-hole courses at Domaine de Saltgourde, rte d'Angoulême, Périgueux, tel: 53530235, 12 km south of Bergerac in the grounds of Château de Sadillac, tel: 53584609, and near Souillac at Lachapelle-Auzac, tel: 65370148.

Swimming – Pools (*piscines*) are to be found in every town and most large villages, run by the municipality. They are clean, noisy and, for the young, very enjoyable. Expect to pay a small entrance fee. An alternative are the many man-made lakes (*étangs*), which have been built for family outings. Pedaloes and small boats can be hired, swimming is encouraged and facilities will probably include a tennis court and café or small restaurant. There are also many small beaches (*plages*) along the rivers Dordogne and Lot, Célé, Vers and Vert.

Riding – There are over 30 *centres equestres* in the region where you can have lessons or hire a horse for the day or week. You can also book all-inclusive equine holiday weeks or weekends with well-trained horse, two large saddlebags, insurance, horse fodder, bed, breakfast and supper. Details from: Tourisme Equestre de la Dordogne, Chambre d'Agriculture, 4-6 Pl. Francheville, 2400 Périgueux, tel: 53092626, and Tourisme Equestre du Lot, BP 103, 46002 Cahors, tel: 65350709. In the Lot there are 600 km of signposted bridle paths and 22 stopover points. Potholing (*spéléologie*) – The region has many deep caves and rock-shafts called *gouffres, igues* or *avens*. If this activity interests you, the Musée de la Spéléologie in Les Eyzies-de-Tayac is a good place to start, tel: 53297842. The leading club is in Périgueux at 38 rue du 26 Regiment d'Infanterie, tel: 53534650. Make sure you get local advice and assistance before tackling unknown holes. Leave details as to your route. The office to write to is CDS, M. Jean Lafaurie, 46150 Catus, tel: 65227049. Also M. Broqua, tel: 65317081. A guided weekend *spéléo* including food and lodging costs 935F.
For the even more adventurous there is parachuting (Bergerac airport), hot-air ballooning (Château de Veyrignac), helicopter tours, and hang-gliding at Cahors-Lalbenque airport.
See **Water Sports**.

Telephones & Telegrams: You will find numerous payphones but the majority require a phonecard. Coin-operated telephones take 1F, 5F and 10F coins. Phonecards (*télécartes*) are available from post offices and *tabacs* and cost 50F and 100F. To use a card phone, lift the receiver, insert card, pull down the handle above it and dial. For coin-operated telephones, insert the money first, then dial. In post offices (see **A-Z**) you can use a metered telephone which lets you make the call before paying. If using a café telephone you may have to buy a token (*jeton*) at the bar. Calls from your hotel room will be charged at a premium. Cheap rates are 2130-0800 Mon.-Fri., after 1400 Sat. and all day Sun. and public holidays. To telephone the UK from France dial 19, wait for the tone to change, dial 44 (11 for USA, 61 for Australia), then the STD number minus the first 0, then the number. To telephone France from the UK dial 01033 then the eight-figure provincial number. You can receive return calls at telephone booths. Telegrams can be sent from a post office or over the telephone by dialling 001111.

Television & Radio: There are six channels on French TV: TFI, A2, FR3, LA5, M6 and Canal+ (the first paying and coded network). News broadcasts are at 0800, 1300, 2000 and 2300. French radio stations broadcast on FM. It is possible to receive BBC Radio 4 by tuning into 1500 m on long wave, and 463 m on medium wave for the BBC World Service.

Time Difference: French standard time is GMT plus one hour and the clocks go forward an hour in summer, making France always one hour ahead of the UK.

Tipping: A 15% service charge is included in your bill at all hotels and restaurants, as is TVA (VAT), so there is no need to leave anything unless you feel the service has been particularly good. If you pay by cash, any small change is usually left for the waiter. Hotel porters expect to receive 10F per item of luggage, chambermaids 10F per day, taxi drivers 10-15% of the fare and hairdressers about 10F.

Toilets: Public toilets are to be found in public parks, in most town squares, at the railway station (SNCF), the bus station (*gare routière*), and of course in restaurants, cafés and bars. Modern unisex steel *cabines* with a 2F fee are replacing the old stand-up, iron-clad WCs which for centuries have been part of the French street scene.

Tourist Information: The Dordogne, with 46 Tourist Offices (often known as *Syndicats d'Initiative*) and the Lot with 33 offices, take tourism very seriously. The offices are usually in the main street, are open Mon.-Sat. and are always helpful with advice, maps and literature. They rarely change money but advise on hotels, restaurants and local excursions, and often arrange town tours.

Périgueux Dordogne Department Office, 16 rue du President Wilson, tel: 53534435.

Syndicat d'Initiative, 1 Ave d'Aquitaine, tel: 53531063.

The offices are close together halfway between the Roman remains in the west and the old town, shopping centre and River L'Isle in the east. Ask for brochure *La Fête en Périgord*. Some town visits are in English.

Bergerac   97 rue Neuve d'Argenson, tel: 53570311.
Town visits, wine region and *bastide* town trips (see **A-Z**).

Sarlat   Pl. de la Liberté, tel: 53592767.
In beautiful 16thC Hôtel de Maleville. Ask for *Informations Générales*. Some town tours in English. Regional tours along the River Dordogne to see castles, and northwest to see troglodyte caves.

Cahors   Syndicat d'Initiative, Pl. Aristide Briand, off Bd Gambetta, tel: 65350956.
Ask for *Vacances et Loisirs*. Tours of *vieille ville*, wine regions, and canoe/camping bookings.

Figeac   Pl. Vival, tel: 65340625.
Ask for leaflet *Figeac en Quercy* in English.

Gourdon   Syndicat d'Initiative, allées République, tel: 65410640.
English-language leaflet *From prehistory to history, Gourdon en Quercy*.

See **Accommodation**, **What's On**.

Tournie, Jean (1652-1702): A master woodcarver of the 17thC baroque style in Gourdon. See his pulpit in the Église des Cordeliers, resting on his statue of Samson; the mantelpiece in Maison des Consuls; and every reredos and most wooden statues in the region! See **GOURDON-WHAT TO SEE.**

Tours: See **Buses**, **Tourist Information**, **Transport**.

Transport: There are air services to the local airports from Paris and Toulouse. Train services on the main line north and south are excellent. However, the best method of transport is by car. The roads are all very good and well maintained but get congested in midsummer, so local bus tours should be considered. Select your interest (prehistory, wine, chateaux, *bastide* towns, pilgrimage sites) and consult the local Tourist Office, SNCF or bus station (*gare routière*). See **Airports**, **Buses**, **Driving**, **Railways**, **Tourist Information**.

Domme

Traveller's Cheques: See **Money**.

Troubadours: In the 12thC Périgord produced a host of romantic ballad-singers, called troubadours, who amused the feudal courts with their wit, poetry, music and songs. Their theme was of pure, hopeless, unrequited love for the (important) ladies of the court. One of the best-known, Bertran de Born (1145-1215), was born at the chateau of Born, near Salagnac, but spent much of his time serenading at the great chateau of Hautefort (see **CHATEAUX-PÉRIGUEUX 2**) and in his spare time freebooting and carousing. Three other well-known troubadours were Bernard de Ventadour, who was buried at Boisseuilh, Guillaume de la Tour, who lived near Ste-Nathalène, and Arnaud de Mareil, born in the chateau of that name in 1150. Elias Carels was born at Sarlat and Arnaut Daniel at Riberac. By the start of the Hundred Years' War (see **A-Z**) the troubadour tradition had died out. See **Eleanor of Aquitaine**, **Richard Coeur de Lion**.

Walking: The French take long-distance walking very seriously. The Grandes Randonnées are well-marked trails which cross the region. The Lot for instance has more than 700 km of signposted footpaths. Footpath maps called *Topoguides* are available in the UK and in France. The GR6 starts in the west and goes through Ste-Foy-La-Grande, Monbazillac, Trémolat, Le Bugue, Les Eyzies-de-Tayac and Sarlat, towards Souillac, Rocamadour and Figeac. The GR5 is also a west to east route following the River Lot towards Cahors. The GR36 runs from the northwest through La Rochebeaucourt, Mareuil, Bourdeilles and Chancelade towards Montignac, Thonac and St. Léon-sur-Vézère, then south towards Monpazier and Biron, Bonaguil, Cahors and St. Cirq-Lapopie. The GR4 crosses the north of the Dordogne department west to east; the GR46 runs along a north-south axis from Brive to the east of Cahors; and the GR651, 636 and 652 are minor variations. The Lot Tourist Office claims that the waymarks are so clear that it is impossible to get lost!

One pleasant way of seeing the countryside is to rent a trained donkey (*âne bâté*), which will carry your family baggage and amuse the children. Three points of departure are L'Anerie Ladevèze, Cours, tel: 65314279; Les Attelages 'La Taillade' at Duravel, tel: 65365353; and Rasseneur, Espinières, Orniac, tel: 65313217. Information can be obtained from the Tourist Offices in Périgueux or Cahors. See **Tourist Information**.

Water Sports: With three major rivers sweeping majestically parallel to each other from east to west – the Dordogne, Lot and Vézère – the region offers superb facilities for a water sports holiday. There are several hundred kilometres of rivers without dams, and several firms offer 2-7 day canoe holidays with tent, mattress, life belts, insurance, canoe-rental and return to the start point by minibus. Canoes can be hired on the Lot at Brengues, Cahors, Cajarc, Figeac, Luzech, Orniac, Puy L'Evêque, St. Sozy, Souillac, Touzac and Vayrac, and on the Dordogne the best sites are at Cenac, Siorac-en-Périgord, St. Vincent-de-Losse and Vitrac. Contact Safaraid, Pl. du Rampeau, 46700 Puy L'Evêque, tel: 65213039, and in season tel: 55288070 (Dordogne and Lot rivers) and 53507264 (Vézère river). MJC, 42 impasse de la Charité, Cahors, tel: 65350643, also arrange canoe rental on the rivers Lot and Célé. Prices vary considerably, starting at about 170F per day, but less per day for a longer rental. Learner courses are available for *initiation au canoe kayak*. See **Sports**.

What's On: Tourist Offices in Périgueux, Bergerac, Sarlat and Cahors publish either a monthly or seasonal guide to all local activities (in French). See **Events**, **Music**, **Tourist Information**.

Wine Festivals:
About 12 June: Bergerac has a procession of growers of Monbazillac wines.
About 9 July: Le Buisson (near Cadouin) wine fair; *23-24:* Sigoulès wine fair.
13 August: St. Aulaye (50 km west of Périgueux) wine and cheese fair; *21:* Siorac-en-Périgord wine fair.
Check beforehand with Tourist Offices as dates vary. See **Tourist Information**, **Wines**.

Wines: East of the Bordeaux claret wine-growing region is a cluster of 93 villages around Bergerac which produce nearly 50 million bottles of wine a year. The climate is mild and the vines are grown on gently-sloping terraces on both sides of the River Dordogne. Two thousand years ago the poet Ausonius declaimed the excellence of the vines and their produce, introduced by the Romans in 60 BC. The young King Henry III authorized the sale of Bergerac wines in England and there has been a steady trade ever since. The four Appellation Contrôllée wines are Bergerac (mainly red, some white and a little *rosé*); Monbazillac (golden white); Montravel (white); and the little-known but excellent Pecharmont red. The best places to buy local wines are at the wine co-op near the SNCF in Bergerac, and various wine co-ops at Monbazillac and nearby Sigoulès. The co-ops offer a wider range to try than most of the individual wine chateaux. See **BERGERAC-EXCURSION 2**.

The rich purple wines of Cahors, established during the late Roman occupation, were favourites with popes and Russian tsars and the English nicknamed them 'black'

wines. Usually they mature for several years and good places to buy them are the large co-ops at Les Côtes d'Olt and Rigal, Château St. Didier, both in Parnac southwest of Cahors. About 10 million bottles are produced each year, and Cahors is becoming a popular wine in the UK. See **Wine Festivals**.

Youth Hostels: About 25 towns in the region have a youth hostel (*foyer des jeunes travailleurs*), usually for ages 13-18, with a maximum of five nights' stay in a dormitory room in any one hostel at economic rates.

Périgueux   Résidence Lakanal, Bd Lakanal, tel: 53078361.

Sarlat   Auberge de Jeunesse (IYHF), 15 bis Ave de Selvès, rte Périgueux, tel: 53594759.

Cahors   Foyers des Jeunes, Frédéric Suisse, 20 rue Frédéric Suisse, tel: 65356471.